Teens' Guide to Adult Skills

Everything You'll Need to Prepare for Adulthood, Independence, and Success!

Kev Chilton

PickWood Publishing

Teens' Guide Series

Also by Kev Chilton

Book One – Teens' Guide to Making Friends

Book Two – Teens Guide to Dating

Book Three – Teens' Guide to Health & Mental Wellness

Book Four – Teens' Guide to Financial Independence

Book Five – Teens' Guide to Adult Skills

TEENS' GUIDE TO ADULT SKILLS

Teens' Guide Book Series

https://kevchilton.com/books

https://kevchilton.com/books

Dedication

With thanks to Beth, whose initial conversations gave me the idea to create this five-book series.

A special thanks to Grace for her meticulous research and invaluable advice, which played a pivotal role in creating each book.

To my good friend, Anna, who kept me sane throughout!

Contents

Introduction

THE UPS AND DOWNS of adolescence have got to end some time, and for most people, that time comes around the age of 18. You're finishing compulsory schooling and you're ready to embark on your next big adventure: adult life! Whether that's going off to university or getting a job and moving into your own place, there are big changes ahead.

You'll no longer have to justify staying up late or why you're having tacos for dinner three nights in a row. No one's going to query why you're binge-watching yet another Netflix show and letting the washing-up pile up. There's nothing quite like being the ruler of your own universe, but all these new responsibilities can be a little daunting. Knowing how to find the area of a triangle isn't going to help you work out which bus to take to get to work on time, and being able to name the countries of Europe won't come in handy when you're planning the weekly shop.

Being an adult takes the skills of being a teenager to a whole new level. You've got to build on what you already know about organizing your life and balancing work and fun with the added responsibility of taking care of yourself and handling new things like paying bills and commuting to work or uni.

It's okay to feel worried about what the next few years are going to look like. After all, they're going to be vastly different from everything you've known so far. No more school lessons and having your life timetabled and organized for you; you're going to be completely in charge of your own schedule from now on. That means, if anything goes wrong—if you're late for work or you forget to turn up for a friend date—there's no one else to blame.

Taking Control

Some young adults can't wait to stretch their wings and fly the nest, but others don't think they'll ever be ready. If you have found being a teenager difficult, you might feel completely unprepared for adulthood. That makes perfect sense—I'm afraid you aren't going to find your anxiety magically melt away on your 18th birthday—but don't worry, there's still plenty of time to work on important skills like being confident or communicating with others.

You might be legally an adult, but that doesn't mean you've stopped growing. Your brain won't even be fully formed until your mid-20s. So, if you can identify the things you're most worried about, you can get the right support to help you. The internet is a good source of information on everything from filing tax returns to changing the fuse in your Playstation, but for advice on how to deal with societal pressure or not knowing what you want to do with your life, look no further than these pages! Over the following chapters, I'll be helping you to brush up on your skills in communication and conflict resolution, letting you in on some of the things that adults have to think about, and sharing some tips on dealing with roommates and how to get any clingy parents off your back.

I left home at 18 to join the police force, and it was a stark awakening. I still felt like a naive teenager, convinced that everyone around me had all the answers and one day they'd discover that I was a complete fraud. I didn't get a gentle transition into adulthood where I felt I could find my way and be allowed to make mistakes and ask for help. As a result, my mental health suffered and my self-confidence dropped to an all-time low and I'm not entirely sure it ever really recovered. I firmly believe that if you land on your feet as an adult, you'll never look back.

If you are comfortable in yourself and you have confidence in your abilities to manage different situations, you're already doing a lot better than most adults I know. Being able to function independently at home, at work, and in social situations is the key to setting yourself up for success. People who can't communicate with others, or who find it difficult to talk to their boss in a different manner to their friends, are always going to struggle making progress at work or making new friends. Employers value social skills like these, especially from employees who work as part of a team or who have customer-facing jobs.

This book is going to take you on a journey from an awkward teenager to a confident adult. We'll start by addressing social skills and self-esteem, then broaden your view of the world and introduce you to new cares and responsibilities that society will expect you to have. After a quick spot of goal-setting and learning how to find your passion, we'll end with some practical information about moving out and moving on from the family home. There'll be joy and sorrow and excitement along the way, but that's what makes it an interesting ride. When you're ready to begin the voyage into adulthood, read on!

ESPECIALLY FOR YOU!

https://kevchilton.com/free-books

Chapter One

Why Communication is Key

IT TOOK ME QUITE a long time to develop a voice, and now that I have it, I am not going to be silent. –Madeleine Albright

Thanks to cell phones, social media, and the internet, it's the easiest it's ever been to keep in touch with others. Have you ever counted how many messages you get sent in a day, or how many new posts from friends you see? Would it surprise you if I told you that number was in the hundreds? And that's on top of all the face-to-face conversations you have with teachers, friends, classmates, and family.

Back when I was young, we didn't have the same technology. If you wanted to speak to someone, you called them on the landline and hoped they were home. Before that, people wrote letters and were happy waiting days or weeks for a response. Now some teens feel pressured to reply to messages straight away or their friends think they're being ignored.

Is this increased communication making us all more social? Not necessarily. In fact, it can cause people to be overwhelmed and feel a sort of social fatigue. It can also make it harder to spot important messages and social cues through the constant noise of information—a bit like trying to shout over music that's too loud. If we're all communicating more but it means less, it's no wonder that some important social skills are suddenly lacking.

Can You Learn to Be Social?

Of course you can! In fact, these were important lessons that used to be taught to young people before they were allowed to interact with polite society. If you've ever watched a period drama, like *Bridgerton* or *Pride and Prejudice*, you'll know that there was a strict social code that everyone had to follow. As the years went by, the rules got watered down and people became more accepting of different behaviors, and people started learning social skills by example rather than in lessons. This meant that you would watch everyone around you who knew what they were doing and copy them.

Why Are Social Skills Important?

Humans are social creatures, and in order to thrive, we don't just need food and water; we need connections and relationships. Close relationships with others help support your mental and emotional health. Good social skills are vital to help you make new friends and stay connected to existing ones. Once you're older, they'll also help you advance in the workplace or find new opportunities.

There are lots of different aspects to social skills; let's take a quick look at some of the most important.

Choosing Appropriate Language and Topics

The way you talk to your friends—and what you talk about—should be different to the way you talk to teachers, your parents, or people you don't know yet. You wouldn't feel comfortable if you were introduced to your friend's dad and he immediately started telling you about how he hated his boss or that he had a strange lump on his . It might seem boring, but sticking to small talk—inoffensive topics like weekend activities, new shops in town, or sports scores—is a good way to start getting to know new people.

Understanding Nonverbal Communication

How you say something is much more important than what you say, and I go into this in more detail in my first book, *Teen's Guide to Making Friends.* Basically, your tone of voice, facial expressions, and posture will all be telling people what you're really thinking, and these are clues you don't get when sending messages or posed videos. If you're talking to someone who doesn't look you in the eye and keeps fidgeting, they might be really nervous, and smiling and giving them some space should help them relax.

Having Empathy and Understanding

Being able to tell what other people are feeling can help you navigate a conversation without causing them to get upset. It's an important skill to have because it builds trust in a relationship. Being empathetic also helps you understand how someone else is feeling so you can predict how they will react to new situations. For example, if a friend tells you they are afraid of water, you probably shouldn't tell a story about the time you saw a shark while swimming in the sea nor should you organize their birthday party at the local pool.

Regulating Your Emotions

Sometimes you'll be talking to people and they'll say something you disagree with or that upsets you. This can happen a lot if you're talking to other people with underdeveloped social skills (like teenagers!) It's important that you try and regulate your emotions so you don't react inappropriately, like punching someone because they insulted your football team.

Negotiation and Cooperation Skills

This one's really important if you're working in a group because everyone will have their own ideas on what role to take and how to work. Obviously, you can't all be team leader or chief presenter, so you'll need to work together to decide who does what. When you get a job, the roles will be more clearly defined, but you'll usually still find yourself negotiating with teammates on how to share the workload.

Some people find that mastering different social skills comes naturally while others need to practice and work at them. Most of the time this can come down to experience—being given good examples in the past that you can learn from and opportunities to participate in different situations as you grow up—but if you're neurodiverse, it can make it more difficult to pick up on some social cues.

Here are some real social situations I've had the misfortune of experiencing. Can you identify which social skills were used—or not used—and what could have been done to improve the scenario?

1. I was with my son at the vet, waiting to have our elderly cat put to sleep. The man next to us commented on our pretty kitty and asked why we were there. When I tearfully explained, he then followed up by asking me why?
2. Sitting in a social space with my friends, someone we have spoken to before—but not for years—walks in and sits at our table. Let's call him Tom. Tom doesn't say anything to any of us but leans over my shoulder to see what we're doing (playing a game). He continues to watch for an hour, not saying a word, but occasionally moving round and leaning over a different person.
3. I had signed up for an extra-credit project and was assigned to a random group of ten. I vaguely knew most of the people in the group, but as we came from different high schools, nobody knew everyone. One girl immediately appointed herself as the group leader, gave her friends the jobs they wanted, and then told everyone else what

she wanted them to do.

Did reading those make you feel a little bit uncomfortable? If so, great! It means you're already starting to pick up on some of the badly used social skills, and that shows that you'd probably behave much better in the same scenario. Let's take a closer look at what happened in each.

1. The man shows a complete lack of empathy or understanding of what would be appropriate in this situation. He also didn't read our body language, which was very closed off and withdrawn. Instead of asking why we were having our cat put to sleep, he should have offered sympathy and then left us alone.

2. Tom made everyone feel very uncomfortable because he kept invading their personal space. If he took notice of our body language, he would have been able to see that and take a step back. He also should have said hi and asked questions rather than just watching us, but of course, we could have taken the lead on that too.

3. It's okay for a confident person to take the lead in assigning group tasks, but the way to do it is by facilitating a discussion and making sure everyone is heard, not by taking complete control. "You can take notes, okay?" is not the same as saying

"would you be happy to take notes?" or "are you interested in taking notes?" The rest of the group should have been more assertive (more on that in a minute) and challenged her.

Activities to Improve Your Social Skills

Just forcing yourself to get out there and talk to more people won't necessarily improve your social skills, as you might just end up rehearsing bad habits. Instead, there are things you can do by yourself to help with skills like regulating your emotions or growing empathy.

Practice trying to see things from other people's point of view. It will help you be more empathetic and understand their feelings and reactions better. Think about a character from a book/movie/TV program that you know well and imagine what they would do in a hypothetical situation. It could be something dramatic—like how Harry Potter would deal with a zombie invasion—or normal and realistic—like how Katniss would react to receiving an ugly sweater for her birthday.

Once that starts coming easily to you, move on to characters you don't know. This means you have to actively look for clues in their dialogue and actions. While watching a movie, randomly pause the action and think about what you think each character would do next. How were they acting before you paused things? If they were angry, do you think they're the kind of character to now become violent, storm off, or burst into tears? Then press play to see if you were on the right track.

Try journaling. You can download an app or buy a notebook that gives you prompts for things to think and write about. This encourages you to reflect on your day, your emotions, and your reactions, and consider what was good and what could be improved. It's a great way to get to know yourself and what your instant reactions are, which can then help you work on finding more appropriate alternatives. For example, if you notice a certain person always gets you riled up, you can prepare yourself with some exit strategies to change the topic of conversation.

Join in with team sports. Working with other people will help you become more resilient and adaptable while also working on your cooperation skills. There are loads of team sports out there that you probably have never thought of, like water polo, volleyball, and ultimate frisbee, and other sports that can be played in pairs, like pickleball, and table tennis.

Go to a show or an improv comedy night. You'll be part of the audience's shared emotional experience, which will not only let you see how others react but will guide you toward the same response. You'll also get to see wonderful examples of body language and emotional expression that are usually more subtle in casual conversations. This will help you identify different emotional responses more easily.

Helping Others Feel Heard

Live theater will also give you a masterclass in active listening. When you have a conversation with someone, you're not just waiting for them to finish talking so that it's your turn again. In order for the conversation to progress and have an impact, you need to register what they're saying. This doesn't just mean listening to their words; it also means recognizing their emotions and understanding what they're expecting from you. Active listening is a skill that encompasses all three of these aspects.

Why bother improving your listening skills? Well, firstly you'll take in a lot more information than before, meaning you'll learn faster and be better equipped for future situations. However, active listening isn't just about you; it's about making the other person feel validated, valued, and heard.

Listening Implicitly

When you listen, whether it's to a person, a movie, a song, or a podcast, it's not just the words that you're hearing.

Listening to the tone of the speaker's voice helps you know how they're feeling. It's why we find it so jarring to listen to an automated voice reading out information—you get the explicit information but none of the implicit information.

What do I mean by implicit information? It's everything that isn't said. It's the shuffle of the feet that means they're nervous, or the raised tone at the end of a sentence that shows they are still questioning whether what they've said is really true. All the little things you can miss if you're "listening" while looking at your phone, thinking about your homework, or watching the television. Here's an example:

Teacher: Ben, have you got a few minutes? I need to talk to you about your assignment.

Ben: Okay. (watches as his friends go off to lunch together)

Teacher: Your opening paragraph is good, it really sets up...

Ben: (Wonders what's in the cafeteria today. Will the guys save him a seat?)

Teacher: ...but then you wander off topic on the second page. See here where you mention...

Ben: Uh huh. (Thinking that, if he has to re-write this assignment, he's going to have to skip practice tonight. Coach won't like that because there's a big game on the weekend).

Teacher: ...so all you need to do is add an explanation about...

Ben: Okay.

Teacher: ...and then two more paragraphs at the end linking them together. Can you manage that?

Ben: (Suddenly panics) Sure.

We've all been there. It's easy to zone out when there's so much else going on in your life. I'm sure the teacher knew Ben wasn't really listening and wasn't at all surprised when he handed back his assignment without making the changes she suggested.

Responding Explicitly

Lots of passive listeners don't take into account what's been said before they launch into their part of the conversation. While you're talking, they're waiting for their time to speak, not fully concentrating on what you're saying. Imagine you've been telling someone about something that upset you, and instead of asking you about anything you've just mentioned—your feelings, what happened, what you need from them—they immediately launch into a story about something that happened to them. This might be their attempt to connect with you, to find a common ground and show they understand you, but the way they do it has done nothing to validate your experience.

Here are two more examples, this time of the same conversation: one shows passive listening and one shows a more active response.

Millie: Are you okay?

Lewis: Not really. It's been a tough weekend. My granddad was taken into the hospital on Saturday. They think it's his heart.

Millie: Oh! That's awful. I remember when my grandma got sick last year, I was really sad. She's okay now though.

And now, here's an example of good active listening:

Millie: Are you okay?

Lewis: Not really. It's been a tough weekend. My granddad was taken into the hospital on Saturday. They think it's his heart.

Millie: Oh! Lewis, I'm so sorry to hear that. How do you feel now? Is there anything I can do to help?

Millie's second response is much better. It takes into account all the information Lewis has just given her—his tone of voice, his emotions, and his words—and she processes this to decide what Lewis needs to hear next. Her comments show she has heard what he said, acknowledged that he might have wanted to talk about it, and that she is willing to help further.

Active Listening in Practice

To show someone that you're listening actively to everything they're saying, try following these steps:

1. Listen for the entire meaning of their words—what is said and the emotion and attitude that comes with it.
2. Try and read their body language and nonverbal cues to get a clearer understanding of their meaning.
3. Respond to their emotions, not just their words. This builds empathy and will encourage them to keep talking.

Remove Distractions

When someone is talking to you, make sure your attention is completely on them. Don't try and look at your phone, tablet, computer, or television at the same time. Put down your book, pen, or anything else you're doing. Look at them—this way you won't miss any nonverbal cues.

Process the Conversation

Rather than just letting their words wash over you, try repeating them back to yourself. This will help you remember the main points, either so you can reply effectively or so you can store the information for later.

Use Your Body Language

Keep a neutral or positive facial expression, like smiling, to show that you're engaged. Rather than interrupting, you can show you're listening by smiling, nodding, or frowning sympathetically at appropriate moments. Encourage the other person to keep talking by using short responses, like "okay" and "mm."

Prepare Your Response

When it's your time to speak, use everything you have heard and observed to decide what kind of response is needed. Demonstrate that you were listening by repeating back important points. Don't be afraid to ask them to clear something up if you don't think you understood—you can repeat back what you think they meant and ask if you're right.

Stay Detached

Don't take anything that's been said personally—even if it is directed at you. The best thing to do is stay calm and keep your emotions out of it. If you've been reading their body language and emotions, you'll be able to see if anything harmful they say is coming from their own hurt feelings or as a defense mechanism because they're feeling scared.

Putting Out Fires

As a teenager, you place a lot of importance on your relationships with your friends, family, and romantic partners. After all, these are the people in your life who help you figure out who you are. They introduce you to new likes and dislikes, support you when you feel upset, and encourage you to follow your dreams. So, when one of these relationships breaks down, it can feel like a piece of your world has been ripped away.

One of the biggest reasons for relationship issues in teenagers is miscommunication. That shouldn't be surprising, considering how teenage brains are in a constant state of flux: always rewiring and reprogramming, so one week you'll see the world from one perspective, and the next week you'll have a whole new one. When everyone's acting like this, it's easy to see how you and your friends could suddenly end up on different pages.

Uh-Oh, Conflict!

Unlike a minor disagreement—like whether basketball is more fun than football or if burgers are better with ketchup or relish—conflicts can fester. They usually happen when one person feels like their view or values is being threatened by those of another; for example, if a friend continues to devalue your decision to be vegetarian by offering you food items they know contain meat products. A conflict is not usually something you can "agree to disagree on," and they don't go away if you just give them a bit of time. Not having strong social skills can make conflicts harder to deal with because you don't feel confident in your ability to talk to the other person about how you really feel.

Conflicts at home can be especially difficult and stressful to manage because you'll probably find yourself up against an adult—someone more worldly-wise, with more authority, and more influence over you. If your adult has under-developed social skills, they might not be able to guide you both toward a clear resolution, meaning you can both get stuck in a conflict rut.

Resolution Techniques

Because conflicts don't go away on their own, there are a number of different strategies that people can use to work toward a clear solution. These are:

- Submission: where one person stands down from the conflict, admits they're wrong, or agrees that the needs of the other are more important than theirs.
    - Beth needs to arrange a time with her project partner Pixie-Iris to finish their presentation. She can only do it after school on Tuesday because she's needed to look after her younger brother on other days. Pixie-Iris has a piano lesson on Tuesday, but after realizing there are no other options, she backs down and agrees to miss one lesson so they can work on their project together.
- Withdrawal: walking away from the conflict and putting some physical space between you and the other person. This gives people a chance to calm their emotions and think more logically.
    - Chantal and her dad have been fighting about Chantal's decision to quit the debate team, even though they reached the regional finals

this year. During a heated argument, Chantal reveals that she's failing chemistry and wants to spend more time studying, which is why she quit the team. She storms off to her room, but an hour later her dad knocks and they talk more calmly. Her dad tells Chantal that he understands her reasons now and he's proud of her for prioritizing her learning.

- Compromise: where both parties come out of the conflict with something they want or agree on, usually by also agreeing to something that benefits the other person.
    - Maxine has just passed her driving test and wants to be able to drive herself to school, but her mom is worried about how dangerous it can be driving through the city. Maxine argues that she wants more independence and she's had enough lessons to know where she's going. They agree that Maxine can drive herself on a Friday when she doesn't have first period so she'll avoid the rush hour. If that goes well, her mom is open to letting her do it more often.
- Standoff: moving away from the conflict by changing the topic of conversation. It won't solve the problem, but it buys everyone some time to

cool down and think things through.

  - Woody and Dane are trying to plan a trip for the football team, but they both want different things. Woody thinks they should go on a summer tour and play some friendly matches against local teams near where they're staying, but Dane wants it to be more relaxed and about team bonding than playing games. They aren't getting anywhere with the conversation, so they agree to do some thinking and discuss it again the following week.

- Third-party Intervention: when you can't find a solution, sometimes the best thing to do is ask someone else to help you. This could be an impartial friend or a trusted adult. They'll listen to both people's opinions and suggest which one of the first three strategies they can see working best. Because conflicts can get very emotional, often asking someone else to mediate is the best way to stop everyone getting even more upset or angry.

  - Lorraine wants to apply for a language degree, but her parents are set on her being a doctor. They refuse to support her decision and threaten to throw her out if she doesn't do as she's told. Lorraine asks her guidance counselor to mediate a meeting between them. She is able to explain the reasons for her choice—she already gets great grades, helpful for all future careers, and is more likely to do well at it as it's her passion—and her parents also get to explain their views—guaranteed job after study, potentially high income, and stability. The guidance counselor helps Lorraine's parents understand that those things can come from many jobs, and also gets Lorraine to understand that her parents are trying to help her do well in the future. Lorraine's parents agree to look at language courses with Lorraine and speak to college professors and careers officers so they can all make an informed choice.

You have to choose the right strategy for your situation, but if you're not sure which to go with, third-party intervention will work in most cases. If, like Lorraine, you need to have a difficult conversation with someone, you might feel more confident having a friend or trusted adult with you. Even if you don't need them to intervene with the discussion, just having their silent support can make a huge difference.

Your Conflict First Aid Kit

If you find yourself caught in a heated discussion and you're not sure how to find a resolution, or even a safe way out, here are some key phrases that should buy you a little time to think and help to calm down rising emotions.

- I can tell that you feel very strongly about that. Let me have a minute to think about my feelings too.
- Can we talk about this again later once we've both had a chance to calm down and think things through?
- I understand your opinion. What do you suggest we do next?
- I understand your opinion, but I disagree. Let me tell you my side.
- I don't think we're ever going to see this the same way. Agree to disagree?

Also, if you know that you have made a mistake and want to take the submission strategy, don't be afraid to acknowledge it. "I'm sorry, I made a mistake/I misunderstood" is a very powerful phrase.

Chapter Two

Believe in Yourself

IT TAKES COURAGE TO grow up and become who you really are. –E.E. Cummings

There's no one on the planet more confident than a happy child. They're always sure good things will happen and have boundless optimism. They will talk to anyone as if they're already a friend and believe that they can write the best story, score the best goal, or bake the tastiest cake. When was the last time you felt like that?

Teens often get stereotyped as moody, grumpy, and miserable, and while you don't all turn into goths on the morning of your thirteenth birthday, it's not a stereotype that's used without reason. Due to the effects of puberty, your brain has to deal with a lot of chemical changes. Entire sections are closed for refurbishment, and while they're out of action, other areas of your brain are responsible for temporarily processing their functions. You start to be driven more by things that are immediately rewarding. You're also suddenly more aware of how other people might view you, as well as consequences of your own actions. These consequences can have positive and negative effects on your self-esteem and confidence levels, and I'm afraid to say that it's much easier to lose confidence than it is to gain it.

Here's an everyday scenario, played out from the point of view of the same character, but at different ages:

Seven-year-old Harriet gets home from school and the house smells amazing. Her mom is cooking her favorite lasagna and it's already in the oven. She's really hungry, but her mom tells her she has to wait, so she goes outside to play with their dog. She's having so much fun she forgets about being hungry. When her mom calls her in, she wolfs down a second helping and declares it's the best meal she's ever had. Of course, she said that about yesterday's dinner too.

Thirteen-year-old Harriet gets home from school and smells the lasagna cooking. She's immediately hungry and becomes overwhelmed by the need to eat something, even though the food won't be ready for almost an hour. She snaps at her mom because there's no way she can wait, snatches a packet of cookies off the counter and takes them upstairs. When it's time for dinner, she only eats half a portion because she's no longer hungry. Harriet immediately feels guilty and knows her mom is thinking about how she's ungrateful, fat, and rude. She goes back to her room and hides from her family for the rest of the evening.

Where Does Confidence Come From?

What does this have to do with confidence? The negative emotions teenage Harriet feels as a result of something fairly small and inconsequential (on a global scale anyway) have knocked her confidence. Next time she talks to her mom, she'll be a little less sure that her mom will react well. Next time she feels hungry, she'll remember the extra cookies and wonder if she's eating too much junk food, which will make her less confident about her food choices and her self-image.

Over the course of a day, there will be many small things that happen to you that will change how you feel about yourself, and therefore, how confident you feel. Your total confidence is made up of three other aspects:

- self-esteem: how you feel about yourself and if you think you add value to the world
- self-compassion: whether you beat yourself up over things that don't work out or treat yourself

with kindness

- resilience: whether you pick yourself up and carry on when something goes wrong instead of going to pieces

If you don't dwell on missed opportunities, are able to plan again after unexpected changes, and know your strengths, it's more likely that you will have high levels of confidence. Confident people are open to trying more things and will believe they can succeed. I'm not saying you'll be able to manifest good grades just by thinking you deserve them—if only!—but by spending less time dithering in self-doubt you will produce higher quality work faster.

By contrast, when you go into an activity with low confidence, you will focus on everything you do wrong, and probably overlook anything that goes well—or write it off as a fluke. By worrying about making mistakes, you won't be fully concentrating on the task at hand, and it's this that makes you more likely to trip up.

Confidence Changers

So, what sort of things can raise or lower your confidence? Often it can be the same thing; for example, your grades at school: A high grade will make you feel more confident whereas a low grade will make you feel less confident. Things like this can also affect people in different ways: You might get a huge boost of confidence from a high grade in a subject you love, but your friend will only get a small one because they already know they're good at that subject.

Things that can positively or negatively affect your confidence include:

- academic results
- achievements as part of a team or in individual competitions
- support from loved ones
- self-image
- interaction with social media and advertisements
- learning new skills
- recognition (with awards) or being singled out (for reprimand)

Here's a further list of things that will negatively affect your confidence. Most teens will experience a couple of these scenarios while growing up, and it'll depend on how resilient you are as to how quickly you bounce back. Some are able to shrug off bullying remarks without letting them leave a mark; others will be dealing with the aftereffects from a family break up well into adulthood. If you do recognize any of these as aspects of your own life, remember that you're not alone and you can always reach out to a trusted adult for help and guidance.

- mental health conditions like anxiety, depression, and ADHD
- physical health conditions like a recurring sports injury, diabetes, or deafness
- feeling under pressure to succeed
- feeling under pressure to fit in and conform
- being bullied
- dealing with discrimination
- family problems
- relationship problems (with friends or romantic partners)
- moving away from what's familiar

If your confidence is already low, negative experiences can have a much greater effect on you than on others. If you've been struggling with low confidence and low self-esteem for a long time, make an appointment with your school counselor or family doctor. They will be able to discuss different support options for you, such as meeting with a regular peer discussion group or exploring a diagnosis of depression.

Developing a Positive Self-Image

No matter how many positive things happen to you, if you don't believe in yourself, you won't feel the confidence-boosting effects. That good grade won't be good enough, the compliment from your friend won't be sincere, and those jeans couldn't possibly be as flattering as they look in the mirror. Anything that doesn't match your own self-image will be discarded by your brain as an untruth.

The reality is that it's your low self-esteem that should be discarded instead. It is possible to love yourself and start thinking good thoughts with just a little bit of extra work. If your self-esteem could do with some self-inflating, try a couple of these exercises. Yes, you will probably feel a little foolish at first, but stick with them, because after a while you'll wonder why you ever thought it was so bad being you.

Envision It!

Create a vision board that represents your aspirations. Fill it with photos, quotes, and positive affirmations. You can create a digital version or go old-school and pin things to your wall, but whichever way you choose, make sure you have it somewhere that you can see it easily. When you're feeling down, lost, or in need of some motivation, spend a few minutes looking over your board, reminding yourself of where you want to be and soaking up the positivity you created.

Celebrate It!

If you find it difficult looking forward, how about creating a collage of your past achievements instead? Pin up grades, photos of times you had fun, team score sheets, or just write up a short journal entry celebrating something you did that you're proud of. It can be as mundane as "I chose a salad with my pizza instead of garlic bread" or "I said thank you when someone told me I looked nice instead of not believing them." Once your wall of achievements and positivity starts to build up, you'll realize just how many good things are happening.

Praise It!

Every day, for a whole month, write down something you like about yourself on a post-it note, fold it up, and drop it into a jar. You can't repeat yourself and you have to be genuine. They can by physical things (I love the color of my eyes) or abstract things (I am a good friend) and you can be general or really specific (I am really proud of my essay on ocean life because I really earned that top grade). You can watch the jar fill up with positive thoughts as a daily reminder that you continue to be awesome.

Guess what you get to do the next month? Shake up the jar and open them, one day at a time. What could be better for building your self-esteem than reliving your own personal highlights?

If in Doubt, Seek a Second Opinion

Seeing the good in yourself can be extremely hard, especially if you haven't had a lot of positive reinforcement from others in your life. However, I bet you could list three great things about each of your friends, supportive family members, and even your teachers (including the ones that give extra homework). You might think your best friend is amazing, but how often do you tell them? As a group of friends, write each other a letter listing what you think are each other's best qualities. After you've read their opinions of you, you might start to see yourself through their eyes.

I recently had to write a personal reference for a close friend, and I sent it to them to read through afterward. They were floored by all the positive things I had to say about them, which I found odd because I assumed they knew how much I valued them. Then it occurred to me, I probably don't say, "I'm so glad I can trust you" or "I value that you're always here for me" on a regular basis, and I really should.

Silencing the Voice in Your Head

Your brain can be your worst enemy when it comes to improving your confidence. You could be walking down the street, minding your own business, and suddenly a random, negative thought will pop into your head. Is that person staring at me because my new haircut looks a mess? What if I get to the mall and my friends are playing a prank on me and aren't really there? What if that A I got on my assignment was a mistake and I really got an F?

We tend to believe messages from our own brains much more readily than those we get from other people. After all, why shouldn't we? Remember what I said earlier about your brain being rewired? While that's going on, it can cause a lot of random thoughts to misfire and make you react to things that aren't really true. Your brain thinks it's trying to help, but this internal critic can lead to a lot of anxiety and worry.

Filtering Out Unhelpful Thoughts

It's impossible to stop these thoughts appearing, even if you're the most zen master of meditation and mindfulness. So, what can you do about them? Learning to deal with unhelpful and intrusive thoughts now will be a skill you can carry throughout your adult life and it's amazingly useful. The best way to start is by critically analyzing them to work out if they are helpful thoughts and based in fact or unhelpful thoughts that come from fear. It's most likely that your brain is trying to tell you something but just hasn't phrased it very well. I once tried to warn a friend that they were about to trip over someone's bag and (most likely) drop their lunch tray, but in my haste the words that came out of my mouth were "look out, food!" It didn't have the desired effect, much like lots of the negative thoughts that get sent your way.

Acknowledge

It's tempting to try and push negative thoughts away, but that doesn't get rid of them. Instead, the thought will pop back up again later, like a piece of homework you were avoiding. Only now, you're more aware of how bad it made you feel, so you're extra anxious to be faced with it again.

Analyze

Focus on how this thought makes you feel. Is it completely negative (I'm too stupid to pass that exam) or more of a mixed deal (I'm going to fail and it's all my fault because I didn't study)? Can you identify whether there is truth behind it—did you actually skip out on studying? Or are you worrying for no reason? Sticking with the example of failing an exam:

- Have you failed other exams recently that have knocked your confidence in that subject?
- Are you feeling guilty for not putting in enough work?
- Was there a particular topic that you struggled with?
- Did you try and get help, but your teacher wasn't available or didn't support you as well as you needed?
- Has something been happening outside of school that made you feel like a failure?

See how that one, simple thought could be just the tip of the iceberg? It's never just as simple as "I'm going to fail;" the idea always has a root in something else.

Replace

Now that you know what your brain was trying to say, you can try and reframe it as something else. Put a more positive spin on things, using accurate information and being kind to yourself.

- I might not do as well on the exam as others, but I've had good grades so far so I should still pass.
- With a little more work on a specific topic, my grade will be fine.
- I know I'm not feeling confident right now, but I have a plan to study before the exam and that will help.

Stubborn Thoughts

Often, it's the thoughts that aren't based on facts that are the worst to try and get rid of. This is because it's difficult to rationalize them, which, in turn, makes it harder to reframe. In this case, try and remind yourself that not every thought you have is going to make sense or even be worthwhile. How many times a day do random song lyrics, memories, or comments just pop into your head? You don't dwell on these, and you shouldn't dwell on unhelpful negative thoughts either.

Tell yourself it's just a thought and imagine it floating away. Will it still matter in an hour, a day, a week, or a month? The chances are that it won't. However, if you find yourself having a lot of negative thoughts, it becomes easier to obsess over them and feel like everything is true. What's the point of letting one go when you know another is just going to take its place? If your negative thoughts are persistent and you feel this way for at least a week, you should reach out to someone for help.

Getting Help

Sometimes, just talking about things with a friend or trusted adult can be enough to lift a dark mood and help you feel better. Other times, you will want to look for some ongoing support. Your family doctor might be able to recommend some talk therapies or sharing groups where you can meet others who feel the same. They might also want to give you some antidepressant medication. This works by helping your brain receive more of the chemicals and hormones that make it feel happy, and this can reduce the number of negative thoughts and bad feelings. Most people who take this medication do so as a temporary measure to help them get through a bad period, and there are few times in your life as unsettling as puberty and being a teenager!

Chapter Three

Being Aware

The first step towards change is awareness. The second step is acceptance. –Nathaniel Branden

Part of growing older is recognizing that your world keeps getting bigger. As a child, you only knew your home and family, then your world gradually grew to include school, friends, and people in your neighborhood. At high school, you're now meeting kids who come from further afield and getting to experience people with a range of different upbringings, family situations, and levels of wealth. With university, work, and the opportunity to travel, you'll start to also meet people who come from entirely different countries and cultures. Why is this important? Not only does it give you a better perspective on things in your own life, but you also get to discover new ideas and ways of doing things.

However, meeting people from different places can have its pitfalls, and this is where you need to learn to be more aware. You've hopefully already started to notice the differences between people in your class and how people behave differently so that no one feels uncomfortable. Maybe you have a quiet, introverted friend who you wouldn't dream of inviting to a rowdy party—that's you showing some social and emotional awareness. Well done!

If you want to get along with people in life, you need to hone your awareness skills. As a toddler, you could get away with throwing a tantrum if no one bought you an ice cream. After all, it's expected that toddlers think only of themselves and not worry about embarrassing their grown-ups in public. Can you imagine the reaction if you threw a tantrum in school because someone took the last slice of pizza? Everyone would stare and be confused because they're aware that that's an unusual reaction for a teenager.

Awareness can be broken down into different types and you'll need to work on all four in order to forge good relationships and be successful and accepted by your peers. Briefly, these are:

- self-awareness: knowing that you exist and therefore can impact your surroundings
- emotional awareness: recognizing emotions

(yours and other people's) and knowing how to manage them

- social awareness: thinking about other people and how they will respond to things
- cultural awareness: understanding the viewpoints and experiences of people from other cultures

You'll develop some awareness naturally just by being in different situations and learning as you go. Other kinds of awareness—like those social skills we've already looked at—can be taught, and lots of people make a conscious effort to learn about other cultures so that they don't make mistakes or accidentally do something rude.

Self-Awareness

This is a really hot topic at the moment, and it's something we all assume we're really good at. After all, you've been aware of yourself since you were a toddler—you can recognize yourself in a mirror, you know that if you push a chair, it will move, and you're absolutely certain that you won't suddenly dissolve or disappear. Awareness of your physical self is one thing—and how weird would life be if we didn't have it?—but self-awareness runs on a deeper level too.

You're more than just a large piece of meat staggering aimlessly around the room, and knowing what makes you a unique individual is very important for self-awareness. What are your values? What do you believe? How does your personality come across? How do your emotions react in different situations? Being able to answer some of these questions can increase your level of self-awareness.

Self-awareness can be further broken down into two more categories: public and private awareness. If you have to stand up in class and read out your work but start to feel nervous or worry that everyone will think it's awful, that's your public self-awareness kicking in. It's the recognition that people are watching what you're doing and (most-likely) judging or critiquing you. This can lead to performance anxiety, but it's also what stops most people from doing crazy and unacceptable things. How much fun does it look in the movies when someone starts a giant food fight at school? No one does it in real life because they have too much self-awareness. They know they'd get in trouble, be teased about it, or maybe no one else would join in and they'd look foolish.

Private self-awareness is more internal, and it's the one people tend to struggle with. It means being aware of your own feelings, what triggers your emotions, and how you interpret different sensations in your body. For example, if you always get butterflies in your stomach before biology class, having self-awareness can help you work out whether it's because you hate the subject, the topic makes you queasy, or you're crushing on your lab partner.

Being a teenager means you probably go through more emotions in one day than adults do in a week. Sometimes it's easy to tell what caused them, but other times you might find yourself lashing out without any idea of why you're suddenly feeling angry. It can be an incredibly frustrating and confusing time, especially if you think you're the only one feeling this way. This is why it's important to start analyzing some of your thoughts and emotions and trying to increase your level of self-awareness—so you can work out what on earth is going on in your brain!

Time to Start Looking Inward

How often do you actually sit down and think about what's happened in your day? Do you ever replay conversations and try and work out which parts of them made you feel happy, annoyed, or angry? Start keeping a self-awareness journal. Write down the different emotions you felt during the day and try and think about what caused them. Include information about how you felt physically—did you start sweating? Get a dry mouth? Feel faint? Was your heart beating fast?

As your journal builds up, take the time to read back over previous pages and see if you can recognize any patterns. Maybe a tingling in your fingers and toes turns out to be an indicator that you're feeling anxious about something. Next time that happens, you can be prepared with a calming strategy so that anxiety doesn't disrupt your day.

Emotional Awareness

Sometimes called emotional intelligence, emotional awareness means being able to tell what different emotions feel and look like. It's crucial for forming good relationships with people. It helps you understand how you're feeling, and that means you can manage your responses. For example, if someone teases you about a poem you wrote, does it make you feel angry, embarrassed, or anxious? If you're angry, you might want to shout at them or lash out. Whereas if you're embarrassed or anxious, you probably just want to get away as quickly as possible. If you don't recognize your emotions, you might not be able to control yourself, and that's how fights start.

Emotional awareness is also important for noticing how other people feel. If you're talking to someone and they start to feel uncomfortable, you should be able to tell by reading their body language, and then change the topic to something else. Being able to identify what others are feeling is called having empathy. You might have heard the expression "put yourself in their shoes," which doesn't actually have anything to do with footwear, but instead means to imagine how you would feel in their situation. If someone new starts in your class, can you empathize with how nervous, unsure, and lonely they might be feeling? What about characters in books or movies? Do you find yourself feeling hope, sadness, and love along with them? These are all good signs that you are empathetic.

Emotional Awareness Is Good for Your Mental Health

Being emotionally aware means you're less likely to struggle with both positive and negative emotions as you grow up. You'll still feel sad, but it won't feel like the end of the world and you'll be able to work through it using strategies like going for a walk, journaling, or talking with others about your feelings. Being able to manage your emotions successfully also builds self-confidence because you trust your own abilities. This self-confidence helps you deal with setbacks and moments of stress, making it less likely that you'll experience anxiety and other low moments of mental health that can be triggered by unexpected events.

Emotional Neglect

Emotional awareness is a relatively recent phenomenon. That doesn't mean we've only just started to care about emotions; it means that people didn't always think that they were important. Negative emotions, like being sad, angry, or frustrated, were bad, and therefore, you weren't supposed to show them or talk about them, and the ultimate goal was to be happy all the time. This is why lots of people were told to keep smiling and get on with things, and it has led to a lot of problems that we're only just beginning to understand.

Not only is suppressing your emotions bad for your mental health, it can affect the people around you. Lots of the adults in your life will not have been taught how to manage their emotions in a way that is helpful, and this means they probably don't have the tools to teach you how to manage yours. Some children today are growing up with emotional neglect: All their physical needs are being met, but no one is looking out for their emotions.

If this is something you're having to deal with, talk to your school counselor or family doctor. They should be able to help you find some resources to develop your own emotional intelligence and point you toward some peer or youth groups where you can share your feelings in a more accepting place.

Social Awareness

You can have social awareness without social skills and vice versa. Being aware of others doesn't automatically mean you have the tools to interact with them as smoothly as you'd like. That's what social awareness is: being able to acknowledge and think about the views of other people, whether that's individuals or groups.

It's easiest to be socially aware among people you know best, like your friends and family, because you have a lot of information about them. Imagine you're trying to arrange a trip out with friends. You wouldn't take everyone out for burgers if you know someone is vegan nor would you plan a hike if someone is in a wheelchair. Being aware of their likes, dislikes, and needs is important in maintaining good relationships.

Another aspect of social awareness is reading and reacting to situations as they occur. Maybe you're all hanging out in the park but one of your friends starts to go quiet and keeps glancing over at another group of teens nearby. You spot their ex-partner in the group and realize they're now feeling very uncomfortable. If you're socially aware, you'd realize that it was time to move somewhere where everyone can relax.

One final aspect of social awareness is knowing that society expects certain behaviors at different times. A lot of the time, this is just being polite and having manners, like shaking hands when you're introduced to an adult, waiting in line for your drinks, and not shouting in the movie theater. It also includes more sensitive actions, such as using the correct pronouns for someone or making adjustments for someone with a disability without asking them a load of uncomfortable questions.

Cultural Awareness

I could have included this under social awareness—because it's really a subsection—but I think it's so important that I wanted this part to stand out. Racism isn't going away, no matter how much we want to ignore it, and it's a fact that so many people who identify as minority races are treated differently on a daily basis. Some of it, like name calling, is intentional and inexcusable. However, a lot of other issues simply come from people not being aware of other cultures, and this can lead to a lot of misunderstandings.

Learning about other cultures can widen your worldview and change the way you see things. If you go through life only knowing what your family and friends—who, in all likelihood, are the same culture as you—tell you, your view will never change. Speaking to others and learning what the world looks like to them can be wonderfully enlightening. It's the difference between staring at your backyard through the kitchen window, and looking at it from on top of your roof: Your view is wildly improved and you can see so much more of what is around you.

Understanding different cultures makes it easier for you to include more diverse people in activities and conversations. Strict Muslim friends may not be allowed to come swimming with you and Jewish friends might not be able to study with you on a Saturday. Knowing this already can avoid you putting them in a situation where they have to refuse an invitation and explain why. Of course, if you do make a mistake, make sure you apologize and let them know that you're still learning about their culture and trying to do better. Most people won't be offended and will be happy to hear that you're growing your knowledge.

Chapter Four

How to Bounce Back

YOU HAVE REJECTION AND you have to learn how to deal with that and how to get up the next day and go on with it.
–Taylor Swift

Even if you are always prepared, life has a habit of throwing you curveballs. There are just too many things that we have no control over. While you're still a teenager, the adults in your life will make decisions that affect you and you'll often have no choice but to just deal with the outcome. It's not that they don't want your opinion, sometimes it just isn't going to make a difference; for example, if one of your caregivers loses their job and now the family has to relocate, knowing that you don't want to move house isn't going to change the fact that it's happening.

When part of your life alters, it can leave you feeling unsettled, especially if it happened suddenly. You were used to familiar routines, locations, and faces, and now you have to get used to something different. Then factor in any emotional upheaval that comes with this new change. It's no wonder that many people find it difficult to cope. Learning how to cope with changes—and especially how to recover when something bad or unexpected happens—is a valuable skill that you're going to need more and more of as you approach adulthood.

Of course, changes can be positive too—a new friend or partner, a bigger house, a job with a higher income, a family pet, etc. Even though these changes disrupt your current routines and the way your life has been, they seem easier to manage because they bring joy. You're happy to adjust to meet these new requirements. But even good changes can feel draining if they happen one after the other. It takes energy to transition from one way of doing things to another, so make sure you give yourself some time for the dust to settle.

Change Doesn't Always Feel Good

Kids are supposed to be resilient and always bounce back from a bad day. After all, how many times did you hurt yourself at school or at the park, only to be excited to go back the following day? It seems unfair that getting older means you find it more difficult to handle the bad things, but it's a side effect of developing a more mature brain.

When something bad happens and forces a change on you, it can feel like the end of the world... and quite often it is. It's the end of your world in its current state; so acknowledge that feeling of loss and devastation and spend time feeling sad and coming to terms with the realization that you can't go back to how things were. Whether it's your caregivers getting a divorce, the end of a relationship or friendship, having to move away, or the death of someone special, you can't be expected to wake up the next morning and act as if nothing has happened.

How to Help Yourself

It's important not to put pressure on yourself during this period of change. Don't force yourself to be okay or impose any deadlines for feeling better—you'll just end up feeling bad again if you fail to meet them. Hopefully, you have people who will support you through this change, but if you don't, it's even more important that you practice self-kindness. Try writing down your feelings and then looking back over them after a week or two. Do you notice any changes already? It might not feel like you've moved on or started to accept things, but re-reading your first thoughts will hopefully show you that you're already starting to adapt.

Something else that can help is sticking to your existing routine as much as possible. Find comfort in the things that are familiar to you and that aren't changing. If you're moving school, don't change the things you do at home. If you always eat pancakes for breakfast and sneakily share them with your dog, keep it up! If you're moving house, but all your stuff is coming with you, there's no reason why you can't still play video games after school or shoot hoops on the drive, if that's how you usually spend your free time.

One of the worst things about change can be getting anxious about the unknown. If you've got a caregiver who's moving out or your family is relocating to a completely different area, you'll have no reference point for what to expect. Some people are happy to adapt to new challenges as they arrive, but other people like to have a plan, and not being able to plan can cause anxiety. If that sounds like you, try and find some ways to bring a little calm into your routine. Go for a gentle stroll, listen to a relaxing playlist, or find ten minutes for a bit of reflective meditation. It's important to keep checking in with yourself and your feelings and not letting your stress levels get too high.

Bend, Don't Break

When change happens, whether you chose it or not, it can cause a lot of stress. Learning how to deal with the stress so that it becomes manageable is a healthy way of adapting to your new reality. It can be the difference between you coming back stronger or feeling like this change has broken you. Typically, teenagers are not always the best at handling stress. Don't take it personally; it's just that your brain is in the middle of changing too. As you mature into an adult, a lot of rewiring takes place inside your brain, and new networks are formed to enable you to think faster and more deeply—it's a bit like upgrading your broadband connection so you can have faster speeds! While this is happening, your prefrontal cortex—where sensible decisions are made—undergoes some of the biggest changes, and therefore, your brain reroutes your decision-making to a different part: the amygdala. The amygdala is in charge of emotions and impulses, so while you're growing up, your decisions tend to be less logic-based, and more instinct-based. That certainly explains why you can eat a whole tub of ice cream to feel good, even though you know it isn't healthy!

Coping Mechanisms

Everyone has different ways of dealing with stress; these are their coping mechanisms. Some are more effective than others because they work to reduce the stress you're feeling rather than just avoiding it. Consider this example:

Tilly and Hattie are sisters and, after their parents separated, they had to move from a big house in the country to an apartment in the city. New home, new school, and new friends—three very big changes all at once, and they're both finding it very difficult.

Hattie likes to sit in the local park and listen to the birds; it helps her relax a little after school. She's also started a social media account to document her explorations of the city and turned her anxiety over new places into a fun activity that's also helping her get more familiar with her new home.

Tilly spends all her spare time on the phone talking to her old friends, but while it used to be nice to keep in touch, she's beginning to get angry when they tell her what she's missing out on. She refuses to leave the apartment with Hattie, instead choosing to stay in her room and binge on junk food.

Hattie has developed some healthy coping mechanisms, but Tilly has not. This means that Tilly is not engaging with her new life and is avoiding the stress it's causing her, rather than trying to deal with it and reduce it. Avoiding stressful situations may make you feel better at first, but the longer you do it, the more stress builds up and you're going to have to tackle it eventually.

I've already written about healthy coping mechanisms in my previous book, *Teen's Guide to Mental Health* (and you can grab a copy if you want to know more about coping with stress and anxiety), but here's a quick summary of some strategies that can help you to cope with changes:

- Find people that you feel comfortable talking to about what's happened. Opening up about your feelings can be validating and will stop you from second-guessing your own behavior. Also, talking to someone about your worries will help you put them in perspective, and they may be able to reassure you that things won't always feel this bad.

- Make time every day to relax in whatever way works for you. Dealing with change is stressful, and as you go through the day, it can feel like you're collecting more and more stress and carrying it around with you. Relaxing will help you put some of it down again, but don't be tempted to just zone out in front of Netflix or scroll through social media; you need to find something actively relaxing, like meditation, breathing techniques, or doing something creative.

- Exercise! Not only is it great for your body; it also produces positive chemicals that clean out some of the negative chemicals like adrenaline and cortisol from your system, leaving you feeling less stressed and anxious. You can join in with team sports or find something to do by yourself. I'm a particular fan of swimming and yoga because I find that both gives my brain a chance to switch off and start chucking out some of the junk that's been building up throughout the day.

- Actively address the root cause of your anxiety—the difficult change you're experiencing—by looking for solutions. Now, you might not be able to magically get your parents back together or prevent the sale of your house, but you can put a plan in place to deal with some of the next steps. Maybe sorting out the schedule for how you're going to spend time with each parent or planning how you're going to decorate your new room will help you feel less stressed and give you something positive to look forward to.

Things to Avoid

There are a number of other coping mechanisms that temporarily make you feel better by avoiding the problem, but these never work in the long run because they aren't helping you adapt to your new situation. These include escapism and isolating yourself, self-soothing by binging on food or television, or acting out and turning to harmful and risky behaviors. If you, or anyone you know, start acting this way, please talk to a trusted adult and seek help to find a better way forward.

Develop a Growth Mindset

I've already mentioned that your teenage brain is constantly changing and redeveloping itself, but despite all of that, your mindset—the way you think—can be pretty fixed. People tend to assume that things are permanent—you'll always be bad at tennis, you'll never like spicy food, you're going to feel heartbroken forever—but the reality is that all these things can change if you put some effort into it.

A growth mindset is knowing that you are in control and you can affect your world. It might take a lot of effort, but you will see improvement. Look at the Grand Canyon: One river carved that out of the rock, very slowly, and over millions of years, but it's a wonderful example of how sustained effort can make real change. You might find something difficult, but having a growth mindset means recognizing that you will find it easier if you take the time to try.

Thinking this way can be really useful when you have to deal with something disastrous. It helps you accept that things will improve and you can bounce back from whatever has happened. View unexpected changes as minor setbacks where you have to refine your plan rather than throw it away and feel lost. This will make you more adaptable and able to deal with changes.

When Support Falls Through

Being resilient and adaptable is so much easier when you have a good support network behind you. This is usually made up of family members and close friends but can also include teachers, sports coaches, and people from your religious community. However, sometimes this support fails you or you aren't comfortable talking to them about a problem that is personal in nature. Don't ever feel like you have to go through a stressful and difficult situation on your own. Here are some other places where you can find support when you need it, such as:

- Your family doctor will be able to listen to your concerns in confidence without passing any information back to your parents.
- The school nurse or guidance counselor should also be able to point you in the direction of local resources. However, because they are part of the school, they have a duty to report any instances where they think you are in danger or are a danger to yourself.
- There are various online charities that offer sup-

port, either specific to your situation or just to teenagers in general. You should be able to find a phone number, web chat, or forum where you can talk to trained volunteers or even join a peer support group.

- You might have an extended family member, like an aunt or a cousin, who you feel able to talk to. Even if they don't live nearby and aren't able to offer physical support, it's always good to have someone to confide in.
- Any trusted adult, especially those who work with children, should find time to listen to your problems and work with you to find a solution.
- If you have a social worker, it's their job to support you, so don't be afraid to get in touch.

Chapter Five

Navigating Different Pressures

WHEN YOU FIND YOURSELF stressed, ask yourself one question: Will this matter in 5 years from now? If yes, then do something about the situation. If no, then let it go. –Catherine Pulsifer

You might have already noticed it, but your life changes a lot as you move from childhood to adulthood. I don't just mean that in terms of how you spend your time and what you're allowed to do, but also that more is expected of you. As a kid, your day is filled with having fun (hopefully) and learning new things (again... hopefully!) The adults around you don't expect much else, except that maybe you'll have good manners and be careful. There's very little pressure on you to do things or behave in a certain way.

As you become a teenager and then an adult, people's expectations of you will change, and there will be more of them. These expectations exert pressure on you: pressure to succeed, pressure to conform, and pressure to comply. Too much pressure and the weight of all these expectations can then lead to stress and burnout if you don't know how to handle them, so it's important to start figuring it out while you're still young. I know that sounds extremely negative—I promise you, not everything about adult life is going to suck!—but many of these pressures are there to help you mature and grow into a wonderful human being.

Evaluating Expectations

I remember the first time I watched *Encanto* with my grandkids and heard the character of Luisa launch into her heartfelt rendition of *Surface Pressure*. Eternal praise must be heaped upon Lin-Manuel Miranda for giving a whole generation the perfect anthem to help explain what it feels like to struggle under the pressures of society and the expectations that other people put on you. These are external pressures—demands that come from other people in your life who want you to behave and act in ways that they deem appropriate. Some of these expectations are entirely fair; for example, your manager expecting you to be polite at work or your family expecting you to be respectful at a funeral. However, just because they're reasonable doesn't mean conforming to these expectations will always be easy. Smiling at customers when you've just broken up with your partner and want to cry is hard.

There's another type of pressure you'll find yourself struggling with, and wouldn't you know it, *Encanto* has a song for that too! Over the course of singing *What Else Can I Do?*, Isabela reveals the pressure she put on herself to be perfect, and by the end of the song, she has learned to give herself a break. Internal pressures are expectations that come from yourself. Often, they're shaped by external influences, but at the end of the day, they are driven and controlled by your own brain. Maybe you push yourself to always get perfect grades or be the best player on the team or always be emotionally available for your friends and siblings. Too often, internal pressures and expectations are unrealistic or unsustainable—a little bit of motivation is great, but make sure your goals are achievable.

External Pressures

Unfortunately, there's not always a lot you can do to moderate or change the external pressures you feel, especially the negative ones. You can't easily walk away from a dominating and controlling parent or leave school just because the teachers think you can work harder. What we're going to look at in this chapter is how to recognize when you're feeling pressure and what you can do to deal with it. That might mean raising a complaint against a manager who expects you to work unfair hours, or it might mean learning to schedule your time better so you don't find deadlines so frightening. I must admit, I'm still working on that last one myself!

Where Do These Pressures Come From?

External pressures and expectations are all around us. Even the adverts we see are pressuring us—you must smell like Johnny Depp or wear the same clothes as Zendaya. In small amounts, they can be motivational or inspirational, but if you don't learn how to manage them, they can add a lot of stress to your life. Here's a quick rundown of some of the different types of pressure you might not even realize you're under:

Cultural Pressure

Every culture has it's own expectations, and this puts pressure on teens to grow up and follow the same path.

You might even feel like you belong to more than one culture, which makes it especially difficult to juggle the expectations because they're unlikely to be exactly the same. You might be expected to wear certain clothing, socialize with similar people, only date people who are "approved" by your parents—or not date at all—and observe cultural festivals and holidays that mean you miss out on things with your friends.

Shazia was born in the United States to Muslim parents. They are pretty relaxed about cultural traditions and let her dress in the same clothes as her friends. She wears a hijab to mosque and when attending cultural events because she understands this is expected of her. Her grandmother is travelling over from Saudi Arabia and will be staying with Shazia's family for two months. She is a strict Muslim and expects Shazia to be wearing a full burqa all the time, which is stressing Shazia out because she doesn't want to have to deal with the comments and questions from her classmates.

Generational Pressure

Have you ever tried to do something and been told, "oh, I wouldn't have been allowed to do that at your age" by adults? Even though the world is rapidly changing and different generations are growing up in vastly different ways, pressure comes from the older generations to conform to the same expectations as they had to. Things like working in a stable job, getting married, having kids, and owning a home are all external pressures that boomers, Gen X, and millennials were told were signs of success, and therefore, must be worked toward, as if they were video game achievements and you couldn't 100% life without them. You might feel differently, and that's okay, but it isn't going to stop your family and older adults in your life from pressuring you into doing well on their terms.

Both of Marc's parents went to college and picked careers where they have been happy and successful. He doesn't have a clue what he wants to do, but they keep talking to him about the importance of a stable career and it's making him feel like a failure who doesn't have his life sorted. His friends are talking about traveling and have invited him to join, but even though he loves the idea, he knows it will disappoint his parents.

Peer Pressure

This one is the junior version of generational pressure, but that doesn't mean it's less stressful to deal with. As if feeling pressure from your culture and the adults in your life weren't enough, you're now also getting it from your peers as well. Sometimes peer pressure can be good and can motivate you to do well—if your group of friends are particularly studious, they will be exerting a good influence and encouraging you to study and work harder. But listening to the wrong peer pressure—"go on, everyone else does it"—can affect your confidence or put you in some sticky situations.

It's the last week of exams and Brooke is really fed up. All of her friends finished their subjects before her, but her Spanish teacher has stuck an exam on the Friday morning. Her best friend Chloe is throwing a party on Thursday night and even though Brooke has told them she can't go, Chloe and the rest of the group keep acting like they know she'll be there. Beth keeps wondering if she should go, even though the exam is important and she wants to do well. She's worried that her friends will stop liking her if she misses the party.

Societal Pressure

Our society seems to have nothing but unrealistic expectations for everyone. One quick glance at social media and you'll see that we're expecting teens to be beautiful (but not slutty), popular (but not fake), thin (yet curvy in the right places), and goofy (but not dumb). It must be exhausting trying to keep up this persona while constantly knowing how far short you fall.

Kimi has just started at a new school and a few of the kids in her class have added her on social media. Kimi is amazed by the number of posts these kids make in a day—their whole lives seem to be online! Kimi notices that everyone seems to post pics all dressed up and in full make-up, so she tries one too to see what all the fuss is about. It gets a hundred likes really quickly. Kimi isn't really into fashion and makeup, but now she feels like she has to keep posting this type of content in order to make friends.

Educational Pressure

We've all had good and bad teachers—the ones that inspire you and those that seem to only care about getting through the lessons as quickly as possible. I'm not making excuses for bad teachers, but there's a lot of pressure on the whole educational system to produce better results year after year, and this expectation filters down to the students. Teachers want you to do as well as you can, and that might mean putting you under a bit of pressure if they don't think your grades are where they should be. You've probably heard a lot already about how employers are looking to hire people with good degrees or the minimum results out of high school you need for different jobs. Whether you're someone who is aiming high or struggling to reach those minimums, you're going to feel the squeeze.

Lennon's older brother was a straight A student, but Lennon saw how hard he had to work to keep it up and he isn't interested in dealing with all that stress, so he gets solid Bs.

Unfortunately for Lennon, his school keeps predicting him As—he and his brother must have got similar baseline scores on some test when they were younger—so his teachers are always hounding him to do better. His English teacher is particularly hard on him and keeps calling Lennon a disappointment and talking about how he is wasting his potential. Lennon used to shrug it off—after all, it was his decision not to be a slave to studying—but recently it's beginning to get him down.

Internal Pressures

All of the external pressures we've just looked at can then feed into the internal pressure that you put on yourself to be perfect, to look perfect, or to please everyone. Not only is it impossible to be flawless all the time, it's unhealthy to even try. When you hold yourself to really high standards, it becomes easier to not meet them, and then you often end up feeling like a failure. This is your self-doubt talking, and it's the enemy of your self-confidence.

Self-Doubt Lives in All of Us

There isn't a person alive who hasn't, at some point or another, felt that they weren't good enough. Self-doubt is a natural part of life, and sometimes it can even be useful because it brings humility and teaches us to challenge our own views and learn those of others. Can you imagine how awful it would be if everyone thought they were right all the time?

Unfortunately, self-doubt can be the loudest when it's being unhelpful, and there are a few different ways this manifests.

- I can't do it, so why bother trying if I'm only going to fail?
- I shouldn't be doing so well at this; someone's going to realize soon that I'm a fraud.
- I didn't study, so it's my fault, and only my fault, if I fail.
- I'm ugly/boring/fat/stupid and no one will ever like me.

Do any of those sentiments feel familiar? Next time you find yourself listening to your self-doubt, try and remind yourself instead of the things you're good at and what you have achieved. Flick back to chapter two and re-use some of those confidence-boosting tricks to send self-doubt back to the shadows.

One of my previous books, *Teens' Guide to Health and Mental Wellness,* goes into more detail about how self-doubt and low self-esteem can cause you to feel anxious and depressed. There's also a lot more information about how to cope with these feelings and some more great (if I say so myself!) advice on how to improve your confidence.

Fueling Your Drive

You'll have noticed that these pressures are all designed to get you to do something in a certain way. However, that isn't always going to be right for you. Some teens feel under enormous pressure to go to university when they know they struggle academically and would be much happier going straight into employment. It's important to listen to these pressures, but that doesn't mean you have to follow them. Instead, take the time to evaluate the sources of your pressures and decide for yourself whether they're worth listening to—in which case you might find your stress levels increasing for a period of time—or whether you should ignore them and choose your own path.

Let's look back at the examples I gave of teens struggling under different external pressures. Can you recognize who dealt with them well, and who could have made a better choice?

- Shazia's culture is important to her as well as her family. Although she identifies with parts of both U.S. and Muslim culture, she recognizes how important it is for her grandmother that she fully embraces her Muslim heritage and she decides that the cultural pressure she feels is justified. She explains to her friends why she'll be wearing her burqa to school and they help her to handle any comments from other students.

- Marc sits down with his parents and explains that he doesn't know if going to college is what he wants. They (surprisingly) agree that a year travelling actually sounds like a good idea. They were worried that he would sit around doing nothing, but travelling is a wonderful experience and they think it will help him to widen his view of the world. Now Marc can't wait to spend six months backpacking around Europe with his friends. He knows he can always apply to college after.

- Brooke gives in to the peer pressure and goes to Chloe's party, but she makes sure her dad picks her up at 11 p.m. She had a good time but didn't sleep very well because she was worrying about her exam. In the end, she got a decent grade on it, but not a perfect one. She gets angry with herself for ruining her perfect record and vows not to go to any more parties until school is over.

- Kimi's mom notices she seems more stressed than usual and Kimi comes clean about the social media pressure. Her mom suggests taking a break from online friends, especially if they aren't satisfied with the real Kimi. She joins the school's LGBTQ+ group and realizes that's where she feels happiest. Kimi still likes other people's photos online, but only posts her true self now, and still gets lots of attention for her pictures.

- Lennon tries to work a bit harder to make his teachers happy, hoping it will stop them hassling him; however, he begins to get anxious before every English class and his grades actually start to slip because he finds it difficult to concentrate. One day his teacher is handing back assignments and tells Lennon that his brother would be ashamed of him. Lennon snaps and shouts back and is sent to see the principal. His parents are called in to discuss his behavior and attitude. Luckily for Lennon, they have his back, and call the school out on the way they have treated him.

Marc and Kimi made choices that stuck with their own values and rejected the pressures that they didn't feel pushed them in the right direction. Brooke and Lennon struggled to process the stresses they were feeling and ended up going along with external pressures that clashed with their own wants. Shazia chose to go along with her pressure, even though it wasn't what she wanted, because she recognized it's importance to others.

She took steps to reduce the discomfort she would feel, therefore managing the pressure effectively.

Chapter Six

Purpose, Passion, and Preparation

One of the greatest struggles of becoming an adult is figuring out what you want to do and what makes you happy. The courageous thing is to stick with it and see it through and see if you were correct. –Kristen Stewart

Children, teenagers, and adults are all driven by different motivators. Although you might not feel like the things that inspire you have changed that much as you've grown older, you might be surprised to look back and see the differences. Children are driven by a quick reward—for example, getting a treat or a sticker for good work—but you probably already know that those things aren't as exciting or motivating as they used to be.

Some people are lucky and they find something early in life that fills them with passion that sets them on a clear path forward. Maybe they want to be a veterinarian or play football and they're able to fill their life with activities around these passions that make them feel happy and fulfilled. More often though, people find smaller pleasures and things they enjoy doing but don't see these are a driving force in their lives. Like the idea that we all have a soulmate out there, our "one true love," there's a prevailing idea that we should all have "one true purpose," but that's a lot harder to achieve than you might think, especially if you don't understand the whole philosophy behind it.

Introducing Your Ikigai

In Japanese culture, the word ikigai (pronounces eye-kee-guy) perfectly sums up this sense of purpose. Described as your "reason to live" or "true path in life," finding your ikigai is supposed to be the way to invite happiness and fulfillment into your life. It's difficult to translate the whole idea and people who have tried have over-simplified it, mostly because they tried to get ikigai to fit in with finding your perfect job, but it's not just about that. Your ikigai is about finding the elements in your life that add value to it.

Here's a good example: Angela has a part-time job where she clears tables at a busy restaurant on Friday and Saturday nights. On Sunday, she has to look after her little brother Ben while their mother works. Angela always takes Ben into town. He loves riding the bus and waving at everyone out of the window. Sometimes they catch a movie; other times they get big milkshakes and drink them in the park. Sunday is always Angela's favorite day of the week. Seeing her brother having fun is her ikigai: the time they spend together makes her happy and she finds looking after him fulfilling and rewarding. It's the reason why she has her job (so she can afford to treat him), and when she's having a really hard time on a busy shift, it's the thought of the fun things they will be able to do with her wages that gets her through.

Your ikigai can change and evolve as you grow. Maybe you'll be able to use it to guide you toward a career—Angela could look into work in childcare, teaching, or as a personal assistant or professional carer—or it can help you find balance and happiness in your personal life. Right now, your passion might be playing football and everything in your life revolves around practice and matches, but in the future, you might realize that it isn't just football where you want to win, and you find other ways to weave competition and achievement into your life.

The Four Components of Western Ikigai

The idea of ikigai was popularized in the western world in the mid-2010s. Like most information that spread over the internet, it was soon doing the rounds as a meme, and that's how most people know it today: a pretty Venn diagram with four different components. This version of ikigai was designed specifically with your work life in mind (I said it was over-simplified and mistranslated), so while it might not bring you personal fulfillment, it's actually not the worst way to evaluate what you want out of a job. It's a very appealing summary because it makes it seem so easy to find the perfect career—all you have to do is work out which parts of your life fit in which circles!

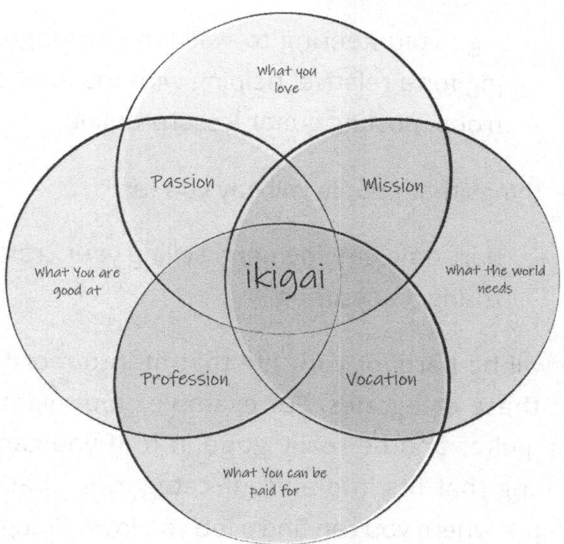

The four different overlapping groups of Western ikigai are:

- things that you love
    - e.g.: playing sports, writing fan fiction, walks in the woods, baking cookies
- things that you're good at
    - e.g.: your top subjects at school, being part of a sports team, getting the lead in the school play, sewing your own clothes

- things that the world needs
  - e.g.: volunteering to walk shelter dogs, caring for a relative, helping with the local scout troop, posting guitar lessons online
- things that people will pay you for
  - part-time employment, selling your crafts, tutoring, babysitting

There will be parts of your life that fit into more than one of these categories. For example, you might love playing guitar and be really good at it. If you can find something that fits into all four categories, that's the sweet spot where you can find a job you love. Going back to my guitar example, if there's a demand for lessons and people are willing to pay you to teach them, it might actually tick all four boxes. But do you only want to be a guitar teacher all your life? Probably not. You'll probably find it enjoyable and rewarding but still want to have a life outside of work, with friends and a family, or opportunities to travel and learn new things. This is where the Western model of ikigai can be restrictive.

In reality, it's hard to find something that satisfies all four components of this model. I get huge amounts of joy and satisfaction from walking my dog or watching my grandchildren play in the park, but no one is going to pay me to do those things. However, I wouldn't consider my life to be complete without either opportunity. I loved my time working for the police; I found the work intellectually stimulating and enjoyed the challenge of getting inside the heads of the suspects I was interviewing, but I didn't want to keep investigating crimes on my days off and I certainly didn't have the athletic ability to become a masked vigilante! As long as you have things in your life that fit into each category, you're going in the right direction.

The Real Meaning of Life

Many people confuse having meaning in your life with needing a purpose that can be quantified. Actually, your true ikigai is all about the little things that bring you joy and help you to grow. This is usually related to something you've personally experienced, and it can happen in the past, (a memory or past event), the present (enjoying hobbies or time with friends) or a plan for the future (your dreams and aspirations). My ikigai is all about helping people. It's what made me successful as a police officer and now it's what's inspired me to write this series of books and help you find yours.

1. Take small steps. You have to recognize that you're not going to be perfect at everything you do, and that's okay. What's more important is to commit to the journey. Even if you're moving for-

ward and improving slowly, you're still growing.

2. Accept yourself. There's no fulfillment in trying to be someone you're not, you'll only end up feeling frustrated. Don't try and follow a path that someone else sets for you if it doesn't fit with your own values and ideals—no matter how proud your caregivers would be if you became a lawyer, you won't be successful and happy unless it's what you want too.

3. Live harmoniously. This can be a strange idea, but what it essentially means is that you shouldn't do what you want at the expense of other people and things around you. Don't neglect your friends by studying all night or upset your neighbors with non-stop drum solos. Also, look for balance in your life, because too much work or study will leave you feeling socially empty, and too much partying will cause your work or grades to suffer.

4. Pursue small joys. Don't just do things because they bring you money or good grades. Yes, these things are important, but they aren't the only important things in your life. Post your artwork on your socials because you enjoyed making it, not to try and get likes and shares. Enjoy the achievement of doing something just for you.

5. Live in the present. Don't always worry about

things that have already happened or try and plan for tomorrow. If you do, you'll miss the beauty of what's going on around you now, and that means you'll also be missing opportunities to have fun. Being spontaneous and joyful is important; it's the antidote to anxiety and worry. If you learn to live in the moment, you'll find yourself feeling calmer and able to enjoy life more.

An Exercise in Self-Reflection

If finding the things you're passionate about was easy, everyone would do it. Quite often we don't really analyze and evaluate how we feel when we're doing things; we don't pay attention to ourselves and our reactions. Luckily, that is something you can learn to do and I'm going to give you a few activities that can help you find the things that spark joy in your soul. By knowing what these passions of yours are, you can weave them into your life, either as a career or to light up your personal life.

Rating Fun Activities

If someone asked you to name things you enjoyed doing, what would be on that list? As children, the answers are going to be fun and instantly rewarding activities, like playing on the swings in the park, eating ice cream, or going swimming. As a teenager, your list will probably include more social and abstract activities, like chatting with friends or hanging out at the park/mall. All of these activities are enjoyable, but they produce different happy hormones in your body, which means your brain receives slightly different messages each time. Socializing with your friends produces oxytocin, a hormone that makes you feel loved and valued. It's a warm, hazy sort of happy feeling that can last a long time, but it's not something that makes you feel passionate.

The hormone you want to produce is called dopamine, and your body creates it when you learn or achieve something. It's what produces that feeling of accomplishment when you finally finish a video game level, help your team with the game, or even get a top mark on your homework. You feel like you've enjoyed an activity and it's been worth it because it activates the reward center in your brain. When you do something you're passionate about, dopamine keeps you focused until the finish line and leaves you feeling satisfied. It's a red hot, sudden and intense feeling of happiness that's over quickly.

At the end of the day, take some time to think back over the stuff you've done. What sort of happy did each activity make you feel? If you didn't do anything that day that you feel passionate about, make sure you schedule something for the next day.

How Do You Know What Excites You?

I'm afraid there is no simple answer here; it's often just a case of trial and error. Start by evaluating the things you already do. Do any of them make you feel like you can't wait to do them again? Another good test I've discovered has to do with your phone—when you're doing something you're passionate about, reaching for your phone will be the last thing you want to do. Did you put your phone down while you were reading a book, playing an instrument, or going for a run? If so, it's likely that these activities are things you feel passionate about. When you're not really invested in what you're doing, it's easy to be distracted by other things, like checking social media or playing a quick game.

If you really don't know where to start—and don't worry, it's quite common to not know what you love to do yet—here are some suggestions.

- Ask your caregivers what you really enjoyed doing as a child. I'm not suggesting you start digging for worms and eating dirt, but it might give you an idea of where to begin. Maybe you were always happiest when creating something, or you always seemed at peace when outside in nature. That could be your cue to find a hobby like sewing, painting minifigures, or sketching, or try outdoor pursuits like hiking, bird watching, or gardening.

- Get each of your friends to introduce you to a new activity, something they love that you haven't tried yet. You might find you're a roller derby prodigy or a natural at break dancing. At the very least, you'll be able to cross off types of activity that you know you don't enjoy, and that information is valuable too.
- Think about things you know you enjoy—can you take them to the next, more exciting level? If you enjoy cooking, how about trying a new type of cuisine or experimenting with creating your own recipes? Do you like traveling to new places? Why not start your own travel blog or social media account to showcase your photos and share your recommendations? If you spend a lot of time watching the latest blockbusters, could you get involved with writing and filming your own short film? You might find that you ignite a passion out of a hobby, simply by investing more time in developing it.

Planning For Your Passions

It's not enough just to know what you're passionate about; you have to make time in your life for it. You might think that'll be easy, but as you get older, there's so much stuff that can get in the way, and before you know it, it's been months since you picked up a paintbrush or baked a sweet treat. Work, study, social commitments, and just being too damn tired will be excuses you'll find for not finding the time to enjoy yourself.

Make a conscious effort to spend at least three occasions a week on your passions. It's up to you how you schedule this because it's going to depend entirely on what your passions are. If you enjoy the rush of a competitive sport, you could watch a game (1), train with a team (2), and have a lengthy debate with friends about your team's chances at a trophy this year (3). Is music more your thing? Spend an hour playing an instrument (1), listen to your favorite album (2), and go to see a local band play live (3).

You don't have to always do three different things; if you just want to play your guitar every evening or spend a whole week knitting a jumper, that's absolutely fine too! It's just my way of showing you a few different options to get you started.

How to Plan for Growth

Western ikigai talks about how you can turn your passions into a career. I'll stress again that this isn't necessary. You can enjoy and succeed at a job that is in a completely different area to your passions and just keep them in your personal life. There are many happy accountants and doctors out there who play saxophone or paint in their spare time. However, you can use your passions and hobbies to start thinking about your personal growth.

What do I mean by personal growth? It's nothing to do with how tall you want to be; instead, it focuses on the kind of adult you aspire to become. It's never too early to think about how you want to develop, and your vision can grow and change as you do. You can have long-term goals and short-term goals, but what's crucial is that you think out some of the steps you're going to have to take to get there.

Writing a Personal Development Plan (PDP)

A PDP is a great way to help you focus on parts of your future. I'll walk you through a couple of examples and show you how easy it can be to create one. You can use them for all aspects of your life, so let's start with a way to develop a passion.

	Short-Term Goal	Action	Short-Term Goal	Action	Long-Term Goal
Passion: Playing Guitar	Learn my favorite song	Buy a copy of the sheet music. Practice for 20 minutes, three times a week	Join a band	Join school music club to meet other musicians	Get paid to play for an audience

There, that wasn't so scary was it? For some reason, the idea of making a plan often causes people to short circuit, but it's really just a glorified to-do list. Here, I've shown you a simple PDP for someone who enjoys playing guitar and wants to keep learning and growing within their passion. The short-term goals are designed to make progress toward the long-term goal, but there's no set time frame or number of short-term goals that must be worked though first. Each short-term goal is paired with a clear action that will help this person achieve them.

As well as improving their ability on the guitar, there are also a number of soft skills being developed here—this is where your hobbies and passions can aid in your growth as a whole person. Practicing and learning a new piece of music shows determination, resilience (for when things go wrong), and taps into that new growth mindset we talked about in chapter four. Joining a club can build your confidence and self-esteem, especially if you get to show off something you're good at.

Here's another PDP, this time focusing more on those soft skills.

	Short-Term Goal	Action	Short-Term Goal	Action	Long-Term Goal
	Step out of my comfort zone more	Say yes to one new thing each day for a whole week	Go to Aaron's party	Agree on a set time to leave with friends so I know how the night will end	Not let my anxiety get the better of me

Again, we've got short-term goals with clear ways of achieving them, all building toward becoming more confident. Have you got a long-term goal that seems too far away? Maybe you want to ask someone out, make it through a class presentation without stuttering and sweating, or have the confidence to try out for the dance team. Try making your own PDP and breaking it down into shorter goals and actions. I promise you, you can achieve anything this way.

Chapter Seven

Learning to Grow

THE TROUBLE WITH NOT having a goal is that you can spend your life running up and down the field and never score.
–Bill Copeland

Once you start to get the hang of creating goals for yourself, there's no limit to how high you can aim. Just remember to keep it realistic! There's no point convincing yourself that you'll only be happy if you can live on Mars and eat chocolate donuts all day without gaining weight. The key to setting goals for yourself is that they have to be achievable. That doesn't mean they're going to be easy or you aren't going to have to put the work in, but it does mean that there's a good chance you'll get there in the end if you plan your path correctly. In this chapter, I'm going to show you how to break those goals down into manageable steps so you can always see the clear path to success.

Be SMART

I didn't just hit the caps lock there because I wanted to shout at you. SMART is a clever little acronym that stands for all the different boxes your goals have to tick in order for them to be meaningful. SMART stands for:

- Specific
- Measurable
- Achievable
- Relevant
- Timed

Let's break these words down even further into more meaningful instructions.

- Specific goals must lay out exactly what you want to do; for example, I want to be able to speak French well enough to have a good conversation.
- Measurable goals need some sort of metric so you can tell when you've reached them. You might decide your French will be good enough if you can pass an exam or after you've studied for

a certain amount of time.

- Achievable goals are realistic goals, taking into account the time, resources, and possibly finances involved. If your school doesn't offer French lessons, can you get them elsewhere? If no lessons are available, will you be able to teach yourself?

- Relevant goals will fit into other things you're doing and help you make progress in other areas too. If you have a trip to France planned, then this is an excellently relevant goal, but if you're going to Italy, maybe not so much!

- Timed goals give you a target date by which you should be able to meet them; for example, before a holiday or if you have a foreign exchange student coming to stay with you. The time needs to be realistic too—you aren't going to speak conversational French by the end of the week, no matter how much you study!

Before you rush off to plan your own goals, here are a few from other teens for you to look at. Can you tell who has created SMART goals and who has got their head in the clouds?

Joanie wants a car for her 18th birthday, which is in eight months time. Her parents have agreed to give her $1,000 toward one if she can match it. She works weekends and is managing to save $75 a month with the rest of her wages going on trips out with her friends.

Rowan wants to lose weight and he's been working with his doctor to create a good plan. Together they have decided that Rowan needs to lose about 50 lbs to reach a healthy weight for his height and body type. He's planning to do this by losing two to three lbs a month through a prescribed diet and walking every day. Rowan has a food diary to fill in and a monthly appointment with the nurse to check his weight.

Mei-lin works in her parent's florist shop but has decided she wants to open her own hair salon instead. She has a lot of experience and understanding of running her own business because her parents have involved her in everything they do. She has found a store to rent and started saving for a deposit. In the meantime, she is trying to persuade her friends to let her practice on them in return for a free haircut.

Luke wants to get fit. After a bit of online searching to find the best way to do this, he's started running twice a week and plans to join the gym in the winter. His nearest gym is on the other side of town and he has to take two buses to get there.

Tyreese wants to go to medical school, but his grades in biology keep letting him down. At the start of his last year of school he sets himself a goal to get them back on track by April. His parents have arranged a tutor for him and his biology teacher has agreed to give him extra work.

How many SMART goals did you spot? Only Rowan and Tyreese have hit all the bullet points—they've made a specific goal with a practical timescale and a way to measure if they're succeeding or failing. Joanie's goal isn't achievable because she isn't going to save enough money to reach her goal within the time she's set. Mei-lin isn't being very relevant or achievable—she might be able to afford the building, but without any skills (and she doesn't mention doing any training), she isn't going to be in business for long. Luke hasn't got any way of measuring how well he's doing—he should define "fit" in terms of being able to run 5k under a set time or something similar—and he hasn't given himself a deadline, which means he could be working on this goal forever!

Learn to Manage Time

Luke isn't alone in finding it difficult to stick to a specific time frame; it's a common issue for teenagers to have. Look at your life so far—everything has been scheduled for you. School and work dictate what time you have to be there, and your caregivers tell you when dinner is ready and when you should go to bed. As you grow older, you get more blocks of free time to manage by yourself. Right now, you're probably spending your free time having fun (I would be!), but soon you'll have to split it between fun, chores, commuting, and all the other boring but necessary tasks of adulthood.

Get Your Priorities Straight

What do you do when you have three or four different jobs to do? Do you crack on and get them done in an efficient manner, or do you sit there paralyzed as you try to work out which to do first? If you (genuinely) answered the first option, I congratulate you, because you're doing better than most of the adults I know! Having a spare hour and needing to choose between cleaning the kitchen, shopping for groceries, relaxing with a book, or organizing your finances can be absolute torment. I know what I want to do (read) and what I should be doing (cleaning), and they're never the same thing. So, how can you learn to organize your time better so that you never feel guilty for relaxing, but you're also not living in filth with empty cupboards?

The key is to prioritize the tasks you have, so that when you come to do them, there's no mistaking what order they need to be done in. Unfortunately, the fun ones usually end up near the bottom of the list, but by making sure everything else is done first—and not wasting time procrastinating about what to do—it means you'll still be able to make time to do them.

Once you set yourself a SMART goal, think about what you need to do every day or week in order to make it happen. These activities should be prioritized below really important things, like assignments or daily chores, but above things that are "wants" rather than "needs," like chatting with friends or playing video games. Looking back at our example teens: Tyreese sets aside two evenings a week specifically to do his extra biology work, one with his tutor and one by himself. He negotiated with his mom that he doesn't have to do his usual chores on those days; instead, he does extra yard work on the weekend. By prioritizing his extra work in his schedule, he won't feel overloaded, he won't struggle to fit it in, and he still has time to relax because he knows that he won't fall behind and need to catch up later.

The Myth of Multitasking

When you know you've got a lot of things to do, it can be tempting to try and bundle a few of them together. There are some times where this can work; for example, reading a textbook while on the bus or studying for your next exam while sitting in the laundromat, but this is because your second activity is filling in the time where you would be waiting around. You wouldn't dare read a textbook while driving a car or studying for your exam while doing the washing up!

Your brain can't actually handle doing two things at the same time. When you think you're multitasking by watching TV while writing an essay, you're actually switching your attention rapidly between both activities. Switching attention like this uses more energy than doing one thing, then the other, and both tasks will end up taking longer. You're much better off writing that essay first and then relaxing with the TV afterward.

Have you ever found yourself accidentally multitasking? Say you sit down to study but then a friend messages you and you send a few messages back and forth while reading your notes. Then you go online to look something up and check a few other things while you're there. It's so easy to do. The best way to avoid distractions and interruptions is to leave your phone somewhere else while you work. If you can't do that, there are apps you can download that block notifications for a set period of time and stop you accessing your other apps. You could also try searching for some music that's designed to help you focus.

Be Flexible

Sometimes you'll know how long a task is going to take, and sometimes you'll have to try and work it out for yourself. Your school probably has a policy of giving you homework assignments that are supposed to take a set amount of time, so you know you should be spending an hour or so on each piece. Now, think about the goal you want to set yourself: How long do you think it will take? One of the hardest parts of goal setting is knowing how long to give yourself.

Let's say you want to learn how to play a particular piece of music on the piano. If you practice every day, it will take you less time than if you only practice once a week. Is two weeks going to be long enough to learn it? How about two months? Do you have a set deadline—is it for a recital or performance perhaps?—or is it more flexible where you can try and give yourself a generous amount of time to achieve your goal in so you're more likely to succeed? If you know you've only got a week and you start missing practice sessions, you're more likely to panic and give up, but if you give yourself two months and manage it in one, you're going to feel such a huge sense of achievement.

How to Handle Feedback

Setting yourself achievable goals and targets is just the start of learning to grow as a person. No matter how awesome you are, you won't get everything right all the time. Part of making mistakes and getting things wrong is that you'll be able to get some feedback, and you can use this to improve things next time. It's basically what scientists, inventors, and other brainy people have been doing for thousands of years. Just look at how cars have improved since they were first invented. Not only are they faster and cheaper to make, they're also much safer and more comfortable to drive. If the designers didn't listen to the feedback from their customers, they wouldn't have made all those necessary changes.

While feedback is an important part of getting things right, that doesn't mean it's always welcome or easy to hear. People love to give their feedback even when you haven't asked for it, and they aren't always thoughtful about the way they do it either. Sometimes you'll have to give yourself feedback, and that can be the hardest of all. We're always far too critical of ourselves and will often also have higher expectations.

Here are a few examples where teens like you have been in situations where they have received feedback and how they've used it to improve their chances of success next time.

Ella goes to the gym three times a week because she is training for a charity half marathon. She often chats to the other people working out, and lots of the staff recognize her and know why she's there. She's been starting her workouts by warming up and then lifting weights before moving on to cardio and a cool down.

Today, one of the staff comes over and tells her that she should be doing the cardio first if she wants to build up her endurance for the marathon. Ella thanks him and incorporates his feedback into her routines by switching around the order in which she does things.

The school science fair is less than a week away and Peaches has just started to work on her project to building a solar-powered oven. It's not going well. The weather hasn't been sunny enough for her to get good results and trying to use a lamp hasn't helped either. She's so frustrated that she throws the whole thing in the bin and bursts into tears. Her dad sits down with her and they talk about everything. He suggests that she should have started planning her project sooner to allow for more time to adjust things that weren't working. At first this makes Peaches angry, but it's mostly because she knew that already and she didn't want to admit that she made this mistake. The feedback won't help her enter this year, but she's definitely going to take notice for next year's fair.

Charlie always loved baking and he's decided to enter a cake in the competition at the local fair. He picks a few of his favorite recipes and invites all his friends over to try them. They're all more than happy to help! Everyone rates the cakes and soon there's a clear winner—the coconut and lime gateaux. Charlie spends a few more days tweaking the recipe by himself and he soon has a version that is moist and sweet with a tangy aftertaste. He's sure the judges are going to love it.

Negative Feedback

Good feedback will focus on what you can do to improve rather than what went wrong. Even so, it can be hard to hear that something you worked hard on hasn't been well received. Especially if you were really proud of your efforts and expecting to hear nothing but glowing praise.

When you get negative feedback, it's still important to say thank you and acknowledge it. Someone took the time to give you notes and help you, even if it wasn't what you wanted to hear. It's okay to take some time away from your project or hobby after getting this feedback, but never let negative feedback stop you from doing something you really enjoy. Even if your artwork or poetry isn't loved by all, as long as you enjoy making it, that's all that really matters.

Take some time before going back and rereading the feedback you received. Now that you're away from the immediate emotional reaction, you'll probably see it in a new light. The things that seems insulting and horrible at first might not sound so bad later. I remember getting my editor's notes from my first book and feeling like an utter failure. After a few days I read them again and realized she was giving me good advice rather than just trying to point out all my mistakes. Stepping away from my defensive gut reaction helped me see the feedback in a more positive light.

Why It's Good to Fail

Sometimes the feedback you receive is terminal. There's no rewriting this essay or tweaking that recipe. It's time to admit defeat. Whether you realize this yourself, or someone else has to tell you, there often comes a time when there's no point continuing. Failing hurts, but it is also proof that you tried something. You took a risk or you persevered with something difficult, and it's okay that it didn't pan out. Your favorite actor has made an awful movie, your favorite singer had a song that bombed; in fact, anyone you admire is going to have more failures in their background than successes. They're a part of life. The reality is, you only need one success, but to get there, you have to rack up a whole bunch of failures.

Why are failures necessary?

- Failure can teach you how to find the strength and resilience to continue.
- Knowing what you don't enjoy or what you aren't good at can help direct you toward what you will succeed at.
- You'll learn how to listen to, and evaluate, feed-

back.

- Learning that it's okay not to be perfect all the time can relieve anxiety.
- They can provide new opportunities and offer you a change in direction.

Knowing When to Give Up

The idea of giving up is always made to sound so negative, but you can waste so much time and energy working toward something that is never going to work. Whether that's a relationship, a hobby, or a school project, there's great power in knowing when enough is enough.

Sometimes the only thing keeping you going is your own ego. You don't want to fail, so you'll do anything to prevent that from happening. But if it's inevitable, you'll only end up exhausting yourself mentally and emotionally and you won't be willing to learn from what happened.

Other times you might feel like you're succeeding when, actually, you're just standing still. If you've been trying something for a while and not been making progress, it's time to admit that this might not be the right path for you after all. You never know; you might try something else and realize it makes you so much happier.

Chapter Eight

A Quick Guide to Adulting

FOR ME, ADULTHOOD IS realizing that there are no grown-ups and everyone else is winging it. –Sarah Beeny

Whether you're looking forward to hitting adulthood or the thought fills you with dread, there's no denying that you are growing older and eventually you'll have to accept that you're now seen as an independent and responsible person. I know, it's a terrifying thought that I struggle with on a daily basis! If society looked inside my head, it would realize that I'm no more confident or capable now than I was 30, 40, or even 50 years ago. I firmly believe that adulthood is a myth!

Adults always look like they have it all together, don't they? As a child or a teen, you'll hopefully have a lot of adults in your life who you look up to and can go to for advice and help. They always seem to have the right answer, but that knowledge isn't instantly downloaded into your brain on your 18th birthday. In fact, the difference between being 17 and 364 days old, and 18 years old, is only so big because of the responsibilities and possibilities that are suddenly thrust upon you by society.

I can promise you that adults are still learning, still prone to making mistakes, and still just as worried about getting it wrong as you are. They just learn to hide it a little better!

Building Connections After School

There is, however, one real difference that it is worth highlighting. As an adult, your brain's ability to change—it's neuroplasticity—slows down after your mid-20s. This doesn't mean you stop learning new things, but it does mean that making changes—for example, changing to a healthier diet—are now just that much harder and less likely to succeed. So, the things that you find difficult as a teen, like making friends or public speaking, aren't just going to go away or be grown out of. That's why I keep pointing out that you shouldn't wait to make changes if you're unhappy about something.

Teenage brains are much better equipped for handling new instructions, whereas adult brains can be stubborn.

School is the ideal place to build up your social skills. You're literally forced to interact with different types of people all day long. Whether it's trying to collaborate with the person sitting next to you or catching up with your friends over lunch, you've got ample opportunities to practice making those important connections with others.

Even if you don't have that many things in common, school provides guaranteed conversation starters. All you have to do is complain about homework or comment that a teacher has been extra mean today, and you're guaranteed to have someone reply. Also, because everyone lives in the same place and many of them will have gone to the same first school as you too, you have built-in experiences in common.

Unfortunately, it's not that easy once you become an adult. The people you work with are unlikely to have the same background as you. Even in a small town, adults will have moved there from all over the country, so you can't rely on being able to make small talk about the new owner of the corner store or how it's a scandal that the library is closing down (yes, I'm afraid those are the sort of things that adults talk about now). Also, while you have to learn to get along with the people in your workplace, that's a very different thing to wanting to become friends and doing things with them in your free time.

You might be lucky enough that, as an adult, you live close to friends from school or college, but how can you grow and develop as a person if you only hang out with people who knew you as a teen? Having a healthy social circle improves your awareness and widens your world-view, so here are some top tips to help you make friends as an adult.

Think Positively

Remember that growth mindset we talked about in chapter four? It's going to come in handy here too. If you close yourself off and tell yourself that it's too late to make new, close friends, you're setting limits on your adult experience. It's never too late to make new friends! Once you believe that your relationships with new people can grow into something more than a superficial work camaraderie, you'll be ready to take a chance on getting close to someone new.

Put Yourself Out There

It might not feel natural or comfortable, but someone has to take the first step toward a new friendship. Start by inviting someone you have a casual acquaintance with to do something with you. If you always see your neighbor jogging on the weekend, ask if they'd like some company next time. Does a work colleague always bring the same kind of lunch as you? Maybe they'd like to come over for dinner, or you could go out together and try a new restaurant.

If someone makes the first move and invites you to join them for an activity, don't automatically say no or try and find an excuse to wriggle out of it. It's probably taken a lot of courage for them to approach you, so make sure you give this fledgling friendship a chance.

Be Open to New Experiences

If you only ever move between your home and your university or place of work, the pool of people you meet is going to be rather small. You might meet your new BFF in the supermarket, but it's not the easiest place to strike up a conversation. If you want to make friends with similar interests, you're going to have to go to places where they'll be! Take a cooking class, join a knitting group, run in the park, or find a local book group. If your workplace offers social activities, take the plunge and go along. You might feel a little awkward at first, but you'll soon get to know people and find you fit right in.

Mine Existing Connections

Who says your new friends have to be completely new? I bet you've had friends try and set you up on dates with people they know, why not see if they can set you up on some friend dates instead? If you move to a new place after finishing school or university, go through your social media friends and see if anyone knows the local area. See if they still have friends living there who might be able to take you out and show you around. Even if you don't immediately become buddies, they'll introduce you to new places and activities that might spark your interest.

Embrace Your Community

Keep an eye out for community events like markets, charity events, or coffee mornings. The people who run these will be on the look out for newcomers and probably make a beeline straight for you to make sure you feel welcome and comfortable. It's likely that the same people or groups will host multiple community events and will have more information about other things they have planned. You might even find yourself roped into helping out—another great way to get to know new people!

Let People In

The real difference between a friend and an acquaintance is down to how comfortable you are letting them see the real you. Every new person you meet starts with a blank slate. They don't know the struggles you went through as a child or a teenager, the different identities you tried on before you found yourself, or the dreams you had to let go. It can be hard to bring those things up again, which is why it's always easiest to go back to childhood friends for advice and support, even if they live hours away. At some point, you need to start letting new potential friends understand a little bit more about where you come from, so they can better understand what motivates and drives you now.

Acting Like a Grown-Up

So, you're out in the world with your new adult friends, working at your new adult job, and living in your new adult home. Does this mean you're going to feel like an adult? I'm sorry to tell you this, but no. However, society is going to treat you like a fully-functioning, totally clued-up adult and expect you to know exactly what to do all the time. It can be really stressful, still feeling like a teenager but knowing that the world expects so much more of you.

Knowing what some of those expectations are can lighten the load a little. It's so much easier to meet targets when you know what they are. Or if you can't—or don't wan't to—meet them, at least you can be prepared for the societal kick back.

The Perfect Adult

Those pressures we looked at in chapter five don't magically go away once you turn 18. In fact, you'll suddenly unlock a whole load more. Adult life today would look almost alien to someone from 100 years ago, yet a lot of society's expectations haven't updated nearly as quickly. You'll still find that you're expected to:

- be in a relationship or actively look for one
- want children, have children, or be planning for children
- want a career and be actively working toward it
- own your own home or be saving toward one
- aim to be smart, go to university, and keep learning
- hit milestones (e.g.: get married) by the "right" age
- be productive, contribute to society, and not make a fuss

Phew, I felt the pressure just writing that list! I'm going to put this next part in a paragraph all by itself so you can see just how important it is. Forget that list and memorize this instead:

There are a million ways to live a successful life. What's right for you is not necessarily right for someone else. Make your own choices with your happiness—not that of others'—in mind.

Don't want kids or want a dozen? Either is absolutely fine, and you don't need to make your mind up at 18 just to keep your Aunt Iris happy. Haven't figured out your sexuality yet? Be yourself; there's no need to choose a label. Happy living at home? Enjoy the cheap rent while you can! No idea what career you want? Try a job, any job, and change it if you don't like it. Exploration and experimentation doesn't end with childhood.

Grown-Up Responsibilities

Having said all of that, there are some things about being a grown up that you aren't going to be able to get away from.

- You're going to have bills to pay. If you use a service, like electricity, internet, or renting a property, you enter into a contract to make prompt and proper payment. If you miss payments, it can have a serious effect on your financial history and will make it harder for you to borrow money or buy things in the future. Nineteen-year-old you might not think it's a big deal to default on a few loans, but 30-year-old you will have some deep regrets when they're refused a mortgage.

- If you have a job, you need to take it seriously. Yes, even if it's boring and menial. Someone has trusted you with an amount of responsibility within their company, whether that means you clean the floors or you run a whole department. They're also paying you to be there, which might be the only motivation you have to stay, especially if it's not a job you're passionate about. Being fired from your job, or frequently changing where you work, isn't going to look good on your resume and you'll struggle to get good references. These can both impact your career well into the future.

- You have to pay your taxes. No one likes doing it, but our taxes pay for a lot of communal services like school and roads, so think of it as a subscription fee for life. If you don't understand how to file a tax return, and you need to do one, ask for advice. Getting it wrong could end up costing you or even result in a criminal charge.

- Look after yourself and anyone (or anything) that you have responsibility for. Your family are hopefully still around to offer moral support, but it's up to you now to take care of the day-to-day tasks. Book your car in for that service, take the cat to the vet for its shots, and make sure you eat enough vegetables and get enough exercise. The better care you take of yourself while you're still young, the fewer health problems you'll get when you're my age.

- Your actions matter. The things you do and say to others will have a lasting impact on a world that is much wider than the school yard. If you are rude to your neighbors or break rules in your apartment block, you might find yourself handed a fine or even an eviction notice. Be kind to them, and you'll find people willing to help you out. Close yourself off from your friends, and they'll realize it takes much less energy to find a new friend than to get to the root of your problems. Make an effort to stay in touch, and they'll be more likely to reach out with support when you need it most.

How to Be an Adult Child

Through your teenage years, you've probably noticed that your relationships with your caregivers and family members has been changing. It might have felt difficult at times, with people imposing strict boundaries and you not feeling like they understand what you need. This is a period in your life where you're forming your own opinions, values, and understanding of the world, a world that is very different from the one that your caregivers grew up in. You feel you're ready to spread your wings, so why does everyone else still seem to get in the way?

Navigating this changing relationship is hard for everyone involved. Your caregivers have spent your whole life looking out for you, protecting you, nurturing you, and trying to prepare you for your adult life as best they can. They will have had to fundamentally change as people in order to do this. Becoming a parent is so much more than just having a small person to feed and clean up after; it's the realization that your needs no longer come first. You would run over hot coals, broken glass, and even Lego bricks if your child was on the other side and they needed you. Watching that child grow into a wonderful, successful, happy, and independent adult is all they've ever wanted, but that doesn't mean they're prepared for it to happen.

A Grieving Process

Many caregivers have good relationships with their children, and they all enjoy spending time together. When these kids (that's you!) become teens, their social circle grows wider and they want to spend more time with friends instead of at home. For you, this is really exciting and a huge leap toward independence. For the adults in your life, it can feel like you're rejecting them or breaking up with them. I still remember the pain of hearing my child tell me they no longer wanted to go to the movies with me, but that they wanted to go with their friends instead. What had once been our fun Friday night treat—complete with popcorn and milk-shakes—was now something they continued to enjoy, but without me. If you've ever bumped into an ex and their new partner, you might have an idea of how that can feel.

Similarly, there must be things you used to do with the adults in your life that no longer happen. Maybe you would all share a hot chocolate before bed and talk about the day, or make an effort to eat together or watch a game, or go to the park. Somewhere along the way, these family activities stopped. Whether you decided you didn't want them, or the grown-ups felt you were too old for them, or maybe your relationships became so strained that they no longer seemed appropriate, there is probably still a part of you that remembers how close you all felt at that time, and wonders where that went.

No matter how difficult the relationship between you and your caregivers has become, they will never stop loving you and wanting the best for you. They might not feel they can reach out, especially if you've ever accused them of being too involved. If you feel ready and you want to reconnect now that the tumultuous whirlwind of adolescence has settled, don't be afraid to take the first step. Why not start by reminding them of a happy memory you have of everyone together? You can use that as a starting block to introduce the idea of doing something else, this time as a group of adults.

Not Letting Go

Whether you're a teenager or an adult, you're still someone's child, and it can be difficult to reconcile the two. If you've got extended family in your life, you've probably witnessed some interesting moments when your grandma is still telling your mom off for cooking the wrong thing, or your grandad won't stop going on about how your uncle is dating the wrong person. Your caregivers are never going to stop having opinions about your life, but there are some things you can do to help draw new boundaries and remind them that, even though you will always be their child, they no longer need to parent you in the same way.

Huge changes in the economy, society, and the world in general have changed the way people parent their children (Jacobson, 2023). As recently as 40 years ago, it was normal for kids to play outside unsupervised all day long with their caregivers only having a general idea of where they might be and what they might be getting up to. A rise in crime (and the media coverage of it), especially toward young people, now means that many caregivers track their children's phones and will call them periodically to check in. Uncertainty over the economy and what the future of the job market will look like has dramatically increased the importance caregivers place on academic achievement. They want you to do the best you can at school because this should make you more desirable for employers later on, but it can also lead you to feeling stressed out and under pressure. Taking this extreme level of control over both your social and academic lives is called helicopter parenting, and it's on the rise. It can be difficult for helicopter parents to hand control over to their children, even once they're adults, because they're so afraid that their children will make mistakes and mess everything up.

When you're an adult, you shouldn't put up with behavior from your caregivers that invades your privacy or erodes your control over your own life. This includes:

- turning up unannounced at your home or letting themselves in when you're not there
- calling you at all times and getting upset or angry if you don't answer
- calling your place of work, your friends, or your landlord
- emotional blackmail (e.g.: telling you to cancel plans and see them instead, otherwise they'll feel

lonely and unwanted)

- trying to influence who you see, where you work, and what hobbies you have
- negative comments about aspects of your life, such as the way you've decorated your home or the job you've chosen to have
- arranging things for you without being asked, like doctors appointments or signing you up for new activities
- stalking your social media accounts to gain information about you

Setting Appropriate Boundaries

The key to having a good relationship with your caregivers once you reach adulthood lies in setting boundaries and making sure they know what is and isn't acceptable. Some families find that this happens naturally, with all adults respecting each other's space and intuitively understanding what kind of contact is needed. For the caregivers who have difficulty seeing their children move away, you might have to stand your ground and spell it out for them. Not in a mean way—there's no need to hurt anybody's feelings; after all, most overbearing parents just want to see their kids happy but don't know how to loosen the reins—but clearly enough that there are no misunderstandings.

1. Start a conversation. Find a time and a place to have a specific chat about this specific issue. Don't bring it up at the end of a visit or in the heat of the moment when you're feeling annoyed.

2. Don't focus entirely on what your caregivers are doing wrong and why it's annoying you. Make sure they know you appreciate their care and attention and you love that they're thinking of you, but then explain that you need them to respect your decisions and your space as well.

3. Ask them if they're okay or if they're specifically worried about something. Their attempts to exert some control over your life might have a specific trigger. For example, if they let themselves into your home while you're at work and refill your food cupboards or do your laundry, you will feel like your privacy has been invaded, but they thought they were looking out for you because you mentioned that money was tight this month. If you know what their worries are, you can show them how you're coping with the problems by yourself.

4. If you need them to listen to your limits or rules, be specific. Make sure they know that there are

specific hours when you're happy for them to call or visit, and others when you're not. If you have changed your diet or routine, be clear about what this means (e.g.: you're no longer eating meat or you're now on the night shift and need to sleep during the day).

5. Encourage them to work with you and plan things in advance. Instead of just focusing on the negatives—when they can't call or visit—follow up with a suggestion to spend the day together at a time that suits you both. Having a child move out, especially if you're the last to go, can leave the family home feeling strangely quiet and empty and it might just be that your caregivers are lonely and lost without you around.

Stick to Your Guns

If you've tried to set boundaries and you find your caregivers aren't willing to listen and the controlling and overbearing behavior continues, you're going to have to be really firm. Don't be afraid to give them an ultimatum—either they respect your privacy, boundaries, and independence, or they don't get to see you. It might sound harsh, but don't forget, it's a last resort. You've tried everything to get them to respect you as an adult and trust that you're capable of managing your own life.

Yes, you'll probably feel horrible and guilty for saying it, but the longer you let your caregivers continue to interfere in your life, the harder it will be to get them to back off. Make sure they know that you love them and they're welcome back once they decide to play ball, and stress that it's their behavior, not yours, which has made you take this difficult step. Hopefully, they will start working with you on building a new relationship based on mutual respect and you can start to reach compromises over allowed behavior.

Not Everyone Gets the Fairy Tale Ending

There will be some of you reading this book who know all too well what it's like to live with caregivers who are controlling; others will live with those who are abusive, neglectful, or unaccepting. You'll be counting down the days until you can leave everything behind and start afresh. It's entirely your choice whether you want to continue contact with family members who have treated you badly. Remember, there are two parties involved in every relationship, and for it to work, they both have to want it to succeed and be willing to put in the work. Taking time away from your caregivers might be right for you. You don't owe anyone a relationship if they're not willing to respect your feelings, your boundaries, or your life choices.

It's your life, don't let anyone else force you to live it differently.

Chapter Nine

End Goal = Independence

THE LEAST REGRETTABLE WAY to live is on your own terms in your own way and for your own cause. –Steven Bartlett

This is what you've been waiting for. The final goal, the entire reason for everything you've done throughout your childhood and adolescence: independence. You've learned all the skills you'll need to make a start, even if you can only cook one dish and haven't worked out how to turn on the washing machine yet. Hopefully, you've also built up a little life experience, either from travelling, working, or taking on responsibilities around the home. However, many people don't feel truly independent until they take the last giant step and set out on their own.

Some people leave for university and never move back home; others do. Some people can't wait to get away as soon as they're able; others are happy to stay in their family home for as long as they can. There are pros and cons to moving out, and it's up to you to decide when is the right time. If you feel comfortable staying at home a little longer and saving up some money, it can make the difference between having to put up with roommates or being able to afford something by yourself. But it does mean that your opportunities for work are limited to what's local, or if you lived in a rural location but your job is in the city, you'll have to cope with a long daily commute. At the end of the day, there's no hard and fast rule that says you have to leave by a certain age; it's down to you and your family to work out the details.

Moving Out

Leaving home can be a really exciting experience: searching for a place to call your own, getting to choose your own furniture and decor, being in charge of your own schedule, etc. Even if it's only a university dorm room rather than your own apartment, you'll still have the freedom to make it your own. But the idea of moving out being an important milestone is a relatively recent one. It's likely that your grandparents didn't move out of the family house until they got married and started a place of their own. In fact, some newly married couples back in the day would have to stay at home until they could afford their own home, which I can imagine was always a little awkward!

A survey of 20-34-year-olds from 2017 showed that more than 25% of them still lived in their childhood home, and up from 19% in 1998 (Civitas, 2019). The main reason? A lack of available and affordable alternatives. Rent and house prices have been rapidly rising since the 1990s, but average income has not grown at nearly the same rate. Thirty years ago, a person could buy a house on a single salary, but now even most couples in their 20s struggle to earn enough to cover their rent, especially in a large city.

So, what can you do about it? Many young adults who decide they want to leave home choose to live with roommates. This means the rent is shared between a group of people so you can afford to live somewhere you could never afford by yourself. This is especially useful in large cities where the majority of jobs are located.

Roommates, Assemble!

You've basically got two options when looking to live with others: Look for adverts where existing groups are looking for an extra person, or agree with a group of friends to all look together. The first option usually works best when you have a job and location in mind and you can choose from what's already out there. Living with existing friends, however, can make it easier to negotiate chores and make arrangements over the shared spaces, but you'll probably all have to compromise on something to find a place that works for everyone's jobs or places of study.

Answering an Ad

The internet is probably going to be your starting point when trying to find someone looking to share their home. You can try asking friends on social media if they know anyone with a spare room and get them to put you in touch. There are also dedicated websites that run ads and match prospective tenants and roommates with groups or landlords who are looking. Some of the ads you'll see are posted by landlords looking to fill an extra room, so make sure you arrange to meet the existing tenants as well before you sign any agreements. Knowing who you're living with is really important because if you all have different values or lifestyles, it might not be very comfortable.

When reading adverts, there are a few things to avoid at all costs. If the apartment is perfectly located and the rent is a steal, it's probably too good to be true, so look out for hidden fees or expectations. Some offer virtual tours or viewings, but you should always visit the place in person too. This will give you a good feel for the area, as well as the property and other tenants.

Here's some top things to remember and watch out for when looking for somewhere to rent with a group:

- You should never have to pay a viewing fee to visit the property.
- Check that the details of the property match it's location. A fifth floor apartment in a converted factory is not going to have leafy green street level views, so if anything doesn't match up, the pictures are probably fake.
- If you're reading the ad through a website like Spareroom or Craigslist, use that platform to send messages to the poster. If they'll only communicate on a private number, they probably have something to hide.
- Look at lots of ads so you know what is a reasonable price and size of property for the area you're looking in. Make sure you know what bills are included and what extras you'll be expected to pay.
- Some adverts specify what they're looking for in a roommate—things like, professional, student, quiet, working day-time hours—so if any of these

don't apply to you, be honest. It might be that the tenants are willing to be flexible if they think you're otherwise a good fit, but they won't be very happy if you move in and they realize they're getting a student party goer instead of a quiet professional.

- Don't go to viewings alone. Take a friend or family member for your own safety. It's unlikely that you're entering the den of a mass murderer, but it's always good to err on the safe side. Also, they'll probably notice things you don't—like a strange smell from the apartment next door or a fire escape that isn't up to code—and you can have a nice coffee afterward and compare notes.

It's pretty much the same when you and your friends are looking for somewhere to live, except this time you'll probably be dealing directly with the landlord or realtor. Make sure you ask to see their ID and that it matches with the person you're expecting to meet. Always read the tenancy agreement carefully and make a note of everything you're liable for. It's okay to want to take it away and have someone else check it over, and you can also ask to make reasonable amendments. Once you sign it, you should also be given a content list of all the items already in the property, from the bed frames to the spoons, and details of the condition they're in. This ensures you can't be accused of scratching something that was already damaged, and it also means you can't pretend that the cool lamp in the living room is actually yours.

Living With Mates

If you're not moving too far from home—or if you're a university student going into your second or third year—you might have some friends who are also looking for their own place. Bunking together sounds like great fun, but it's not just an extended sleepover with your BFFs. It's worth remembering that some of the best qualities in your friends might be the worst qualities in a roommate. You love that they can play all your favorite songs on their guitar, but it's not so great when you're trying to study or nurse a headache. Or maybe it's you who'll be throwing a huge sports party, but they need to study.

Other things to consider when choosing friends to live with:

- Do you share the same standards of cleanliness?
- Are you all able to split chores equally?
- Does anyone have any allergies or dietary requirements that mean you all need to make adjustments?

- Are all the bedrooms roughly the same size or will someone feel like they haven't got a fair share?
- Do you all earn a similar income?
- Are any of you dating, likely to start dating, or do you have dating history?
- Does anyone have a romantic partner who is likely to spend a lot of time at your home?
- Does anyone have any pets?

None of these should be deal breakers, but it helps to be aware of the kind of things that can cause problems further down the line. If you discuss everything before signing the paperwork—and you're all happy with the arrangements—then there's no reason why you can't all have a lot of fun and enjoy the freedom of living together without any caregivers in sight.

Setting House Rules

Of course, that freedom doesn't mean that you all live like animals; your new home still needs a set of rules. If you're joining an existing household, they will already have their rules in place and you should find out what they are before you sign your lease, just in case there's anything there that you don't agree with. If you're starting out together, it's important that you and your roommates come up with the new rules together so that you're all on the same page.

These rules will be different from those you had to live under when you were growing up. I'm not suggesting you insist on everyone being in bed by 11 p.m. or not allowing anyone to take visitors into their bedrooms. Instead, your new house rules should focus on how people treat the shared areas of your home—the kitchen, bathroom, and living area.

Here's a few ideas to get you started:

- Design a cleaning rota that everyone is satisfied with and make sure you stick to it. Go with whatever works for you. Some people like to take responsibility for all of the washing up if it means they don't have to vacuum; others prefer to take it in turns with everything.

- You might find it helpful to agree on a curfew time for using the shared areas, especially on a weeknight. Either insist that all visitors are gone by a reasonable hour or make sure that they stay in their host's room. Don't forget to include a way to ask for exceptions; for example, if someone's having a birthday party. If you know in advance that it's going to be noisy, you could make arrangements to stay somewhere else, as long as it wasn't every week.

- Set rules about what property is communal and what isn't. The living room TV might be shared, but maybe the Xbox isn't. Some people don't mind everyone using their cooking equipment, but others—for example, if they're vegetarian—will want to keep theirs to themselves. It might seem silly having to keep multiple pots and pans in the cupboards, but if it's important to your roommates that their stuff isn't shared, you have to respect that.

Feels Like Home

Your own place is going to feel a little strange at first. It's perfectly okay to feel homesick and take a few weeks to settle in. A really good way to help everyone feel at home is to start some new traditions. You might all have some from your own home that you want to introduce everyone to, or perhaps you could come up with some new ones as a group. Here's a few budget-friendly suggestions to get you started:

- One person cooks, or brings takeout food, for the whole household every Friday. It's a great way to share favorite recipes, plus you're guaranteed a night off from cooking a couple of times a month.
- First Saturday of the month is a PJ day! Everyone brings their blankets into the living room and you

all watch trash TV and eat junk food in your night clothes.

- When someone in the household has a birthday, everyone else gets to wake them up (at a reasonable hour!) and bring them their favorite breakfast in bed.
- Start a regular movie night complete with popcorn and giant sodas. Choose a different theme every month and take it in turns to pick a movie that matches. It could be "movies that you wouldn't watch with grandma," "worst miscast romantic lead," or "movie I most wish I was living in."

Freedom Comes With Responsibilities

You might think you know what you're going to have to deal with once you move out. People have spoken to you about rent and utilities, the importance of budgeting, and eating healthily, but it's one thing to know this in theory and another to live through it. Would you know what to do if your toilet suddenly overflowed or you realized you didn't have enough money in the bank to make your rent payment? Do you worry that you might get your budget wrong and have nothing to eat for a week except rice and cornflakes?

Adulthood means living with an overwhelming amount of responsibility on your shoulders. On a basic level, you have a responsibility to look after yourself, a responsibility to your landlord to treat their property well, and a responsibility to your place of work to perform all the duties they expect of you. These are things that you should be well prepared for thanks to your education and family upbringing. After all, I doubt your caregivers allowed you to destroy furniture or your teachers permitted you to blow off class on a regular basis.

If you fail at some of these responsibilities, you'll end up with more problems than just a bad grade or detention. I'm afraid that you're in the real world now and there are much greater consequences for messing up. Here's a quick rundown of your new responsibilities and what can happen if you fail them.

Financial Responsibilities

If you're employed, you've got to pay your taxes. The systems are different for different countries, so I won't get really specific here, except to say that in the UK, taxes are calculated by your employer and taken from your paycheck (unless you're self-employed) and in the US, you have to calculate and file your own tax assessment forms. The best advice I can give is to make sure you talk to someone who can show you how to do everything right. That could be a paid financial advisor, someone from payroll at work, or a colleague or family member who has a lot of experience. You can also find information online and your local government will probably have leaflets or web pages that will talk you step-by-step through the entire process.

If you don't pay enough taxes, the government will contact you to let you know and request that you make an extra payment. Occasionally, they will contact you to tell you you've paid too much and they'll send the extra back! If you still don't make the payment, they can issue a fine or take you to court. You could find yourself looking at a prison sentence or having your assets seized—where the government takes your belongings up to the value of what you owe. Mind you, this is the final step in the process and you have to have really screwed up to get to that stage. Read your mail, pay your taxes, and let them know if you're struggling and need help, and you'll be fine.

Work Responsibilities

When someone employs you, they'll give you a list of duties you're expected to carry out in return for the money they're paying you. You'll also have to abide by workplace rules like being polite to customers and not stealing someone else's lunch. Do a poor job, and you could find yourself in a disciplinary meeting where your manager will talk you through how to improve. If your behavior doesn't improve, the company can let you go. Your job might not have been inspiring, but it was probably paying for rent and groceries, so it's not a good idea to get to this point.

If you love your job and want to succeed, take the initiative and see if there are training courses available to you that would mean you're able to take on new responsibilities or move into different areas of the company. Managers love people who take the initiative and want to invest in their growth (more on that in a minute).

Contractual Responsibilities

You'll find that you will sign a lot of contracts as an adult. Every time you want to use a service, like electric or the internet, someone will shove a long contract in your face. You should read it, although I know most people probably won't, but the basic thing to understand is that if you stop paying for the service, it will be shut off. If your contract is for an object, such as a mobile phone or a rented house, the company will want to reclaim it. They won't care that you've made most of your payments—you can't take back 20% of a phone after all—so you need to know that if you miss payments, you'll not only lose the object itself but all of the money you've already paid will be wasted.

You'll get regular bills and updates from your utility companies, but the easiest way to pay for all of these is to set up a direct debit from your bank account. That way the money is paid out automatically and you don't need to worry about missing a payment if you're a bit forgetful or go on vacation when one is due. Some companies will shut off your gas/electric/water/internet as soon as you miss one payment; others might send you a few "overdue" notices first. As with your taxes, if something happens and you can't afford the payments, speak to the company as soon as you can. They'd rather change your payment plan and help you make reduced payments than have to write off everything you missed. Also, missing payments on accounts like this will show up on your credit score, making it harder for you to borrow money in the future.

Personal Responsibilities

Now that you're on your own, there's no one nagging you to go to bed before midnight or making you eat your vegetables. If you want to sit around watching late-night TV until 3 a.m. every day while only eating instant noodles, that's up to you. However, you'll soon realize that your caregivers were telling you these things for a reason, because after a few days of very little sleep and bad food, you're going to feel rotten. In order to function properly at your job and enjoy your social time, you need to look after yourself. That means getting a good amount of sleep, eating meals that actually have a nutritional value, and moving your body further than from the bed to the sofa.

Of course it's okay to have a lazy day or eat junk food, especially if you've had a long working week and you're exhausted. You just have to make sure that it's not happening most days. If it is, it might be worth having a quick mental health check to make sure you're not feeling depressed, and if you are, talk to your doctor. Take your health care seriously, as being mentally and physically fit is the only way you're going to manage to juggle everything else in your life.

What Do You Owe Society Anyway?

There are also wider, less tangible responsibilities that make the difference between you being a great adult, an ordinary adult, or one of those adults that everyone rolls their eyes at and crosses the street to avoid. I'm talking about social responsibilities.

The society that you live in is made up of everyone who takes part in it. You can interact with society as much or as little as you want, but regardless of how involved you are, you still have to live in it. Why does that matter? Because your society can change according to the people who influence it. Socially responsible people can make a caring society, one where people look out for each other, volunteer to help out in times of need, and where everyone feels safe, regardless of their differences. Those who aren't can make a society that breeds inequality, where some people are persecuted and looked down on, and everyone acts in their own self-interest. Which society would you like to live in?

I'm not saying you have to spend all your spare time volunteering in the soup kitchen or litter picking in the park, but if you want to live somewhere nice, be prepared to contribute and do your fair share. Stand up for people who can't defend themselves, join the neighborhood watch, throw your trash in the bin rather than on the ground. Taking responsibility for the way that you act when out in public makes your society a nicer place for everyone.

A Responsibility to Grow

Your learning doesn't stop when you leave school, most of it just becomes less formal. If you continue studying at university or take a job where you're learning a new skill, you'll still have a lot of guidance from teachers and other professionals. In fact, you should be able to develop new skills through work—called professional development—for the whole of your career. From learning how to use a new IT system to courses on leadership and team management, you'll be able to upskill and put yourself on the line for promotions and pay rises.

Even if you don't take these opportunities, you'll learn new skills just by doing your job on a regular basis. Spend a few weeks working in customer service and I guarantee you'll work out what phrases make customers feel heard, what winds them up more, and what magical words can end an argument in an instant. That's the benefit of experience. No one goes through life without growing and changing, and it's up to you to decide how you want to influence those changes.

Your biggest responsibility as a newly formed adult is to yourself. I don't mean you should ignore everyone else and only do what you want, otherwise you'd probably never get out of bed. Instead, for the first time, you are the only person who can influence your personal development. It's you who gets to decide what path you want to take in life and how you get to travel it. Do you want to focus on your career, your family, or having as many eye-opening experiences as possible? Where do you want to be when you're 40, 60, or older? You might have no idea of the specifics right now, and that's absolutely fine, but I bet you know that you don't want to still be sharing a rented apartment with someone who leaves hair all over the shower and always eats the last bagel.

When I joined the police, I knew I wanted to make a difference to my community, but the only experience I got at the start was dealing with minor complaints and standing around on the street waiting for someone to steal something or knock an old lady over. It wasn't very exciting, and I knew that I would still be there in 10 years time unless I took it upon myself to find a better direction. I started talking to police officers in other departments about their jobs and then asked to go on a couple of training courses so I could learn some new skills like interview techniques and a bit of basic psychology. Then I took other courses that qualified me for investigating serious crime. It wasn't like the movies where a grizzled old cop on the verge of retirement plucked me from the rookies because they "saw something special in me." I had to take charge of my own career development, and I'm extremely glad I did.

Owning Your Decisions

We've talked about responsibility, but I haven't yet brought up your newfound accountability. You see, not only are you responsible for the decisions you make now, but you're also accountable for the results, good and bad. Here's a small example:

You get a last-minute invitation from a friend on Wednesday evening who suddenly has a spare ticket to a gig, but it will mean that you're home later than usual. What do you do? Any decision you make is going to have both positive and negative consequences that you will be held accountable for. If you go, you'll have a great time, but will you be tired at work on Thursday and could that affect your performance? You'd only have yourself to blame. If you don't go, you'll get a good night's sleep, but will letting your friend down affect your friendship? Maybe you won't be invited the next time and you'll feel hurt not to be asked. Sorry, I didn't say being accountable would be fun!

It's things like this that mean people are often reluctant to make decisions, especially potentially life-changing ones. Choosing between pizza or pasta for dinner is less daunting, but even this can cause some people major anxiety. Before you get too worried about all these upcoming decisions, try and keep the following in mind:

- Don't overthink the consequences. It's far too easy to imagine the worst—or the best—outcome. Instead, try and think of the most realistic. If you're overtired at work, you'll most likely look a bit dozy, rather than being instantly fired.

- Trust your instincts. If an idea feels wrong, but you can't put your finger on why, that doesn't mean you're being irrational or illogical. Don't do anything that doesn't feel right. You don't need to justify your decisions to others or go along with them just because they want you to.

- Always think about how other people will be affected by your decision. I don't mean you should always make the choice that doesn't upset others, but consider whether any hurt you'll cause will be worth it. People at work will get over it if you leave or take an extended leave of absence, but will your friends and family feel the same if you prioritize work over them?

- Don't worry about making the wrong decision; the outcome is rarely irreversible. Everyone makes mistakes; they're an important part of the learning process. You can always make an apology or ask for a second chance.

- Learn to accept the route you've taken. Unless you have immediate regrets, in which case you can try and change things, you'll find many things to be excited about and move forward with. It could be a career change, moving to a new city, or breaking up a relationship that wasn't making you happy. Each decision you make opens new doors; don't focus on those that you've closed behind you.

Did you enjoy the book?

Please take a moment to leave a review, as it can greatly benefit the book's visibility. Your review not only supports me, the author (for which I am eternally grateful), but also helps guide other readers searching for a similar book to discover it and has the potential to help someone benefit from the advice offered.

Thank you, your support is greatly appreciated

Kev

Conclusion

So, there you have it! The biggest secrets that all the adults are hiding from you have now been revealed! Basically, most of us are just winging it, getting through each day on a mixture of experience and some good social skills we've picked up along the way. You're never done learning and developing yourself as long as you stay open to the idea of making changes. In my time, I've seen new policing techniques introduced, new technology trying to make my life easier (sometimes it makes it harder instead), and I've had to get used to living in a society where the definitions of things like gender, sexuality, and equality have changed beyond all recognition. If you don't adapt and change with the world, you'll end up feeling left behind.

The same is true of that giant leap from teenagehood to adulthood. There will be people from your high school who refuse to move on, who cling to the idea that they can be their 18-year-old self forever. You'll see them at your high school reunion, still making the same jokes about the teachers and daring each other to pull the fire alarm. Staying still is a choice, but learning how to grow and move on is a better one.

It's never too early to start thinking about what path you want to take in life. There's no need to have it all figured out right away, but a vague direction is a good start. Are you heading for further study? Do you value getting life experience, perhaps volunteering abroad, or travelling to new countries? Or can you not wait to dive straight into work and start putting your skills to the test? The more you know about yourself and what you want from life, the more likely you are to find it.

So, teenagers, go and discover your passions. Find a way to impact the world and leave your mark, whatever that might look like. Your future is right ahead of you and you can shape it into anything you want. All you need is a little confidence and a lot of drive to succeed.

References

American Psychological Association. (2020, June 1). *Resilience for teens: 10 tips to build skills on bouncing back from rough times.* https://www.apa.org/topics/resilience/bounce-teens

Astorino, D. (2023, May 17). *9 tips for managing negative thoughts.* One Medical. https://www.onemedical.com/blog/mental-health/managing-negative-thoughts/

Bell, S. (n.d.). *SMART goals.* Mind Tools. https://www.mindtools.com/a4wo118/smart-goals

Cherry, K. (2024, May 9). *What is self-awareness?* Verywell Mind. https://www.verywellmind.com/what-is-self-awareness-2795023

Confidence: pre-teens and teenagers. (2024, May 5). https://raisingchildren.net.au/pre-teens/development/social-emotional-development/confidence-in-teens

Confidence and self-esteem – for 11-18 year olds. (n.d.). https://www.mind.org.uk/for-young-people/feelings-and-experiences/confidence-and-self-esteem/

Confident Teens. (2024, January 16). *3 ways a growth mindset builds resilience in teens*. https://confidentteens.co.uk/3-ways-a-growth-mindset-builds-resilience-in-teens/

Cowan, K. (2022, November 10). *Dealing with feedback: the five-step plan to positively tackle criticism of your work*. Creative Boom. https://www.creativeboom.com/tips/dealing-with-feedback/

Cuncic, A. (2024, June 18). *How to stop negative thoughts*. Verywell Mind. https://www.verywellmind.com/how-to-change-negative-thinking-3024843

Emotional intelligence. (2023, June 30). https://kidshealth.org/en/teens/eq.html

Erieau, C. (2020, August 17). *55 best stress quotes*. Driven. https://home.hellodriven.com/articles/55-best-stress-quotes/

Freier, A. (2023, March 6). *Overbearing parents as an adult - how to deal?* Harley Therapy. https://www.harleytherapy.co.uk/counselling/overbearing-parents.htm

Gallo, A. (2024, January 2). *What is active listening?* Harvard Business Review. https://hbr.org/2024/01/what-is-active-listening

Garis, G. M.. (2019, August 8). *Whoever said "quitters never win" is obviously unfamiliar with the superpower of giving up*. Well+Good. https://www.wellandgood.com/when-to-give-up/

Gonzalez, M. (2024, March 29). *What's the difference between internal and external pressures and how do I deal with them?* Bloomerang. https://bloomerang.co/blog/whats-the-difference-between-internal-and-external-pressures-and-how-do-i-deal-with-them/

GoodTherapy. (2023, December 4). *Coping mechanisms*. https://www.goodtherapy.org/blog/psychpedia/coping-mechanisms

Hackett, L. (2021, April 27). *10 social expectations and why it's OK to ignore them*. Ditch the Label. https://www.ditchthelabel.org/ignore-social-expectations

Importance of cultural awareness: everything to know. (n.d.). https://www.getimpactly.com/post/importance-of-cultural-awareness

King, A. (2024, August 19). *10 self-esteem activities for teens & questions*. Carepatron.

https://www.carepatron.com/guides/self-esteem-activities-for-teens?gad_source=1&gclid=cj0kcqjw3zaybhdrarisapwzx8py8yqzhge01ftew4d0s6fxsyhdnnfp3b0awnensalh2qyz4tr5araaaqtqealw_wcb

Litner, J. (2023, April 5). *Dear Boomers, Please Stop the Pressure. Love, Millennials.* Embrace Sexual Wellness. https://www.embracesexualwellness.com/esw-blog/2017/06/14/a-note-to-boomers-from-millenials-stop-the-pressure

Making your own decisions - 8 powerful decision-making tips. (2024, February 23). https://www.1vibrantlife.com/making-your-own-decisions/

Manderson, L. (2021, October 28). *Try this if you're struggling to find your passion*. Tiny Buddha. https://tinybuddha.com/blog/try-this-if-youre-struggling-to-find-your-passion/

Metcalf, M. (n.d.). *Ikigai meaning: 5 steps to unlocking your life's joy*. Marlee. https://getmarlee.com/blog/what-is-ikigai

Miles, M. (2024, July 9). *How to make friends as an adult and why it is so hard*. Betterup. https://www.betterup.com/blog/making-friends-as-an-adult

Miller, H. (2022, February 28). *How I found my passion as an adult (and why it's so important)*. The Everygirl. https://theeverygirl.com/how-to-find-your-passion-as-an-adult/

Mind Tools Content Team. (n.d.). *Active listening*. https://www.mindtools.com/az4wxv7/active-listening

Myers, C. (2024, June 3). *How to find your ikigai and transform your outlook on life and business*. Forbes. https://www.forbes.com/sites/chrismyers/2018/02/23/how-to-find-your-ikigai-and-transform-your-outlook-on-life-and-business/?sh=2c41f5b12ed4

Nathaniel branden quotes. (n.d.). https://www.brainyquote.com/quotes/nathaniel_branden_163773

O'Bryan, A. (2024, July 17). *How to practice active listening: 16 examples & techniques*. Positive Psychology. https://positivepsychology.com/active-listening-techniques/

1m more young adults living with their parents than two decades ago. (2019, June 6). https://www.civitas.org.uk/press/1m-more-young-adults-living-with-their-parents-than-two-decades-ago/

Osei, A. International Students House. (2023, November 28). *Managing roommate relationships: tips for a harmonious living experience*. International Students House. https://www.ish.org.uk/managing-roommate-relationships-tips-for-a-harmonious-living-experience/

Peer pressure. (2024, May 3). https://kidshealth.org/en/teens/peer-pressure.html

Perry, E. (2022, September 14). *What is self-awareness and how to develop it.* BetterUp. https://www.betterup.com/blog/what-is-self-awareness

Pierce, R. (2023, October 18). *13 practical time management skills to teach teens.* Life Skills Advocate. https://lifeskillsadvocate.com/blog/13-practical-time-management-skills-to-teach-teens/

Positive Action Staff. (2023, September 14). *Social awareness: an introductory guide.* https://www.positiveaction.net/blog/social-awareness

Price, C. (2020, August 24). *Parenting teens.* Hey Sigmund. https://www.heysigmund.com/strengthening-teens-social-conversation-abilities/

Raypole, C. (2021, June 17). *How to set boundaries with your parents (and stick to them).* Healthline. https://www.healthline.com/health/mental-health/set-boundaries-with-parents

Safety tips for room seekers. (n.d.) . https://m.spareroom.co.uk/content/info-tenants/safety-tips-for-room-seekers/

Segal, J., Robinson, L., & Smith, M. (2024, August 21). *Conflict resolution skills.*

HelpGuide. https://www.helpguide.org/articles/relationships-communication/conflict-resolution-skills.htm

SEL for students: Social awareness and relationship skills. (2024, March 20). https://ggie.berkeley.edu/student-well-being/sel-for-students-social-awareness-and-relationship-skills/#tab__1

Sutton, J. (2024, August 6). *How to create a personal development plan: 3 examples*. Positive Psychology. https://positivepsychology.com/personal-development-plan/#how-to-create-a-personal-development-plan

thegrownupschool. (2023, March 22). *30 best adulting quotes to make you feel better about growing up*. The Grown-up School. https://thegrownupschool.com/adulting-quotes-to-make-you-feel-better-about-growing-up/

Toso, C. (2018, May 17). *Societal expectations of young adults*. Medium. https://medium.com/@catharinetoso/societal-expectations-of-young-adults-7987f93253d

25 inspirational quotes to build confidence. (2024, February 9). https://www.rebelgirls.com/blog/25-inspirational-quotes-for-girls-to-build-confidence

Vallejo, M. (2024, June 16). *Top 5 characteristics of a growth mindset*. Mental Health Center Kids. https://mentalhealthcenterkids.com/blogs/articles/characteristics-of-a-growth-mindset

Vallejo, M. (2023, November 21). *20 social skills activities for teens*. Mental Health Center Kids. https://mentalhealthcenterkids.com/blogs/articles/social-skills-activities-for-teens#20-social-skills-activities-for-teens

Vidojevic, A. (2021, November 30). *Conflict resolution phrases to use to diffuse conflict at work*. Pumble. https://pumble.com/blog/phrases-to-use-to-diffuse-conflict-at-work/#perfect-phrases-for-conflict-resolution-at-work-and-those-to-avoid

Webb, J. (2022, September 26). *3 challenges for kids whose parents lack emotional intelligence*. Psychology Today. https://www.psychologytoday.com/gb/blog/childhood-emotional-neglect/202208/3-challenges-kids-whose-parents-lack-emotional-intelligence

Weinstein, T. (2024, January 3). *How to help teens build emotional intelligence*. Newport Academy. https://www.newportacademy.com/resources/empowering-teens/teen-emotional-intelligence/

When self-doubt consumes you – identify and stop it. (2024, February 27). https://minddoc.de/magazin/en/self-doubt/

Whitlock, C. (n.d.). *Social skills for teens: a concerned parent's guide*. Healthy Young Minds. https://www.healthyyoungminds.com/social-skills-for-teens/

Why failure is a good thing for students. (2019, February 3). https://www.tutordoctor.co.uk/blog/2019/february/why-failure-is-a-good-thing-for-students/

Williams, C. (2020, September 14). *5 ways to help teens cope with change*. Parent Cue. https://theparentcue.org/5-ways-to-help-teens-cope-with-change/

Wisner, W. (2023, May 26). *How cultural awareness can improve your relationships*. Verywell Mind. https://www.verywellmind.com/cultural-awareness-importance-how-to-develop-it-7500316

Wooll, M. (2022, February 2). *The secret to finding your passion isn't looking, it's doing*. BetterUp. https://www.betterup.com/blog/how-to-find-your-passion

About the Author

HAVING A STARK CHOICE of fighting teens on the city streets or helping them find their way in life, Kev Chilton knew which way he wanted to go!

For most of his working life, he was an inner-city cop and detective, concentrating on murder, gun crime, and other serious offences.

However, he joined the police as a 16-year-old cadet and early in his career, he was tasked with helping young offenders, which quickly became his speciality. He noticed that by simply listening to the problems young people were concerned with, the majority were prepared to listen to him back. He built trusting relationships with most, who were happy to listen to and act on his advice. Many responded positively, and they moved confidently into adulthood.

Throughout his police service, he arranged youth clubs, attended schools where he gave talks and maintained an open-door policy, encouraging any young person with a problem to approach him privately afterwards. He also set up and operated specialist juvenile squads geared towards helping those who had gone off the rails. The results were excellent, and he was never happier in his job than when he could redirect a young person's life onto the right path.

It was a fulfilling time in his life, and it helped him understand the constantly evolving challenges teenagers face as they transition to adulthood. More specifically, as times change, so do the needs and circumstances of young people. Choosing the path of mentorship over the chaos of city streets, he has dedicated his journey to helping teenagers, steering them away from conflict and towards a brighter future.

Today, he is proud to utilise his extensive experience to make a positive impact. He is particularly attuned to the unique issues that young people are currently grappling with, and one of his main goals is to bridge the gap between them and the adults in their lives.

Through this series of his guidebooks for teens, Chilton has become an international, award-winning author, and a beacon of support for teenagers and the adults regularly involved with teens.

Today he lives in a converted barn in the beautiful East Kent countryside where family, walking and writing are a big part of his life, and can be reached at :

https://kevchilton.com

STAY IN TOUCH

Join our Newsletter School 'n Cool and become part of an amazing community, offering valuable content for Teens, Parents, Teachers

https://kevchilton.com/contact

https://kevchilton.com/contact

Teens' Guide Series

EVERYTHING A TEENAGER NEEDS to tackle the significant challenges and opportunities of adolescence can be found within this series. From friendships and mental health issues to finding employment, managing finances, and developing adult skills, these five books offer practical guidance for teenagers to navigate these crucial years with resilience and strength.

The Teens' Guide Series of books has everything you'll ever need to navigate your teens.

Teens' Guide Book Series

Book One

Teens' Guide to Making Friends

Do you find it hard to start conversations or watch others make friends effortlessly? Maybe you just feel awkward and unmotivated. Don't worry—those days are over!

Teen's Guide to Making Friends offers strategies to help you talk confidently, navigate social situations, and handle mistakes without stress. This book will boost your social confidence, giving you the tools to create engaging conversations and build new friendships. Inside, you'll discover how to:

- **Overcome insecurities and become a more confident you**
- **Understand why adults don't always get your struggles**
- **Become your best self, moving forward**

Grab your copy of Teen's Guide to Making Friends.

Book Two

Teens' Guide to Dating

Are you a teen looking to build healthy relationships, set boundaries, and stay safe while dating online or offline? *Teen's Guide to Dating* is here to help you.

Dating can feel overwhelming, whether you're navigating crushes, breakups, or looking after your own safety. Learn how to find the right partner, create meaningful connections, and stay safe. Inside, you'll discover:

- **How to know you're ready to date and build confidence**
- **Ways to set boundaries, get consent, and confidently communicate your needs**
- **Tips for LGBT+ dating and different stages of relationships**
- **Safe sex practices, conflict resolution, and handling breakups**

Teen's Guide to Dating gives you the tools to not only enjoy your relationship but also become the best version of yourself. Ready to start your journey? Read now!

Book Three

Teens' Guide to Health & Mental Wellness

Do you ever feel overwhelmed, wondering why life affects you more than your friends? Your feelings are valid, and *Teen's Guide to Self-Care and Wellness* will help you understand and manage them.

Life's stresses can take a toll, but with the right tools, you can navigate them effectively. In this guide, you'll learn to:

- **Identify negative mental health indicators**
- **Master the key ingredients for mental wellness**
- **Use physical strategies to improve mental health**
- **Provide first aid for anxiety and depression**
- **Build your own personal wellness toolbox**

Learning to manage stress now will make life easier as you grow. Start your journey to wellness with this guide today!

Book Four

Teens' Guide to Financial Independence

Are you a teen seeking financial independence or a parent wanting to guide your teen? *Teen's Guide to Financial Independence* is your go-to resource for building a successful career and managing your money with confidence.

This comprehensive guide will teach you essential skills for employment and wealth-building. Whether you're just starting or need guidance, this book will be your companion throughout. Inside you'll learn how to:

- **Prepare for the world of work and apply for various jobs**
- **Create a compelling resume and excel in interviews**
- **Master budgeting, avoid scams, and handle credit cards wisely**
- **Balance work and life, and plan for university expenses**
- **Understand investing, saving, and hidden fees**

Start to manage ***your*** finances and secure ***your*** future, now!

Book Five

Teens' Guide to Adult Skills

Ever wondered what secret adults don't tell you about the real world? Find out what that secret is in *Teen's Guide to Adult Skills!* Step into adulthood with confidence and learn how to navigate life's challenges! Inside, you'll discover:

- **Activities to improve social skills and resolve conflicts**
- **Strategies to boost self-confidence, develop a growth mindset, and handle pressure**
- **Tips for building emotional and social awareness, and connecting after school**
- **Ready-to-use methods for discovering your passions and creating your own personal development plan**
- **Tools for setting SMART goals, time management, and handling feedback**

Discover your potential and successfully embrace your journey to independence.

Get Teen's Guide to Adult Skills today!

https://kevchilton.com/books

Made in United States
Orlando, FL
08 December 2024

55198044R00104